# GIANT PANDAS

# GIANT PANDAS

BARBARA RADCLIFFE ROGERS

MALLARD
PRESS

**A FRIEDMAN GROUP BOOK**

Published by MALLARD PRESS
An Imprint of BDD Promotional Book Company, Inc.
666 Fifth Avenue
New York, New York 10103

Mallard Press and its accompanying design and logo are trademarks of
BDD Promotional Book Company, Inc.

ISBN 0-792-45242-9

*GIANT PANDAS*
was prepared and produced by
Michael Friedman Publishing Group, Inc.
15 West 26th Street
New York, New York 10010

Editor: Melissa Schwarz
Art Director: Robert W. Kosturko
Designer: Susan E. Livingston
Photo Editor: Christopher Bain
Photo Researcher: Ede Rothaus
Production Manager: Karen L. Greenberg

Typeset by Marx + X Myles Graphics Inc.
Color separations by Universal Colour Scanning, Ltd.
Printed and bound in Hong Kong by Leefung-Asco Printers Ltd.

# DEDICATION

To my brother Charles, who gave me my first panda, with love and fondest memories

# ACKNOWLEDGEMENTS

In the writing of a book, there are always people who offer their time and knowledge to make the book a better one. I am most grateful to Don Reid of the University of Calgary, George Schaller of the New York Zoological Society, Ed Schmidt of the Brookfield Zoo in Chicago, and Rich Block of the World Wildlife Fund for their considerable help and encouragement and to the Friends of the National Zoo for the loan of photographic material. A special word of thanks goes to my friend Judy Maine, who generously shared her extensive knowledge of the world of zoos and animals in the wild. Her help saved me many "wild panda chases" in the course of my research. And to Ruth Maine, who knows the best route to every zoo, without whose directions, my daughter and I never would have found the panda in Paris. My appreciation to Delta Airlines for providing transportation on their new trans-Atlantic routes. And to my daughter Lura, whose unfailing good company made our travels in search of pandas a lot more fun.

—Barbara Radcliffe Rogers

# CONTENTS

INTRODUCTION ▪ 8

*c h a p t e r   o n e*

## MEET THE PANDA ▪ 14

# INTRODUCTION

"The giant panda is not only the precious property of the Chinese people, but also a precious natural heritage of concern to people all over the world."
—World Wildlife Fund

The giant panda has always been an enigma. Elusive in the wild, it was, until a century ago, unknown outside the mountains of Szechwan in China. Difficult to breed in captivity, even the panda's zoological classification puzzled scientists: Was it a bear or a raccoon relative? And now, its numbers dwindling alarmingly, the panda presents the greatest dilemma of all—how to save it.

Questions about the giant panda continue to puzzle zoologists, conservationists, zookeepers and the many others who have made the welfare and preservation of this endangered mammal their business. To the nonscientific world, the panda is perhaps the most endearing of all creatures. Knowing its family tree or understanding its sex life isn't necessary to love this roly-poly, furry clown and enjoy its antics.

Within the hundred or so years that the giant panda has been known to the Western world, it has become the favorite stuffed toy of children on all continents. No other animal captures the attention of the press or the imagination and affection of the public quite like the panda, whose arrivals, births, and slightest activity make instant headlines.

Now an international symbol of endangered wildlife, the giant panda is a fitting representative of all the wild creatures of the earth, drawing our attention to the environmental problems that face wildlife everywhere.

© Chase Roe

"By saving the panda, which is a symbol of world conservation, we express our commitment to and faith in the future."
—Dr. George Schaller, New York Zoological Society

# ELUSIVE IN HISTORY

Although written records as far back as the twelfth century B.C. mention the panda, and later references indicate that it was a treasured possession of emperors and other people of importance, the panda is almost entirely missing from Chinese art and literature until very recently.

There are no early drawings or paintings of the panda. Although other animals were depicted in porcelain, bronze, silk embroideries, paintings, enamels, and papercuttings, the panda was not. Only in the twentieth century, when the rest of the world fell in love with the panda, did it become a popular subject for Chinese art.

Chinese folklore is particularly rich in animal stories and legends, but tales of the panda are few and geographically limited, although in ancient times the panda's range included much of southern China. It appears only rarely in a few more recent children's stories and in mythology only among the minority peoples of the Tibetan borderland. Tibetan herdsmen tell the story of Losang and her three sisters, young shepherdesses who were killed while trying to save a panda from the attack of a leopard.

The then white bears held a solemn funeral honoring the girls. According to Don Reid of the University of Calgary, a leading panda expert, the story goes like this: "The pandas wore black arm bands in mourning, the dye from which ran with their tears and spread as they hugged each other and rubbed their eyes. Hence their coloration. The pandas turned the girls into a mountain with four peaks so that future generations of pandas would remember their heroism. The Four Girls Peaks still look down upon the pandas in Szechwan's Wenchuan County, near the present-day Wolong Reserve. When the panda was spoken of

*In early Chinese literature giant pandas were known as the* bei-shung, *which means "white bear".*

at all after that, it was called the spotted bear or the white bear."

Although other animals were hunted by the local tribesmen, pandas were not. The rare reports of panda skins describe them hanging on the wall of the home of a prominent local person. Pandas did not attack livestock, and when they were occasionally found raiding a beehive, they were most often chased away without harm.

Theodore Roosevelt, Jr., who hunted panda with his brother Kermit for the Museum of Natural History in New York, confirms that the Lolo (or Nosu), a local tribal group, would help West-

thing. Furry pandas with straps on their paws now hug school children as backpacks, while others cover their heads as winter hats. Plastic pandas float around bathtubs holding soap, and velour pandas top pencils and cling to lapels with spring-clip legs. There are panda tote bags, neckties, and even panda shower curtains.

The idea finally found its way back to China, where artists now depict pandas in all mediums, from brush painting and silk embroidery to the popular folk art of intricate paper cutting. The Chinese government, as part of a program to educate its people about their unique wildlife heri-

© Ellen Silverman

(Left) From t-shirts to pot holders, pandas adorn almost any object imaginable. These are just a few of the panda offerings available at the National Zoo in Washington, D.C. (Below) Sir Peter Scott, one of the founding directors of the World Wildlife Fund and an accomplished wildlife artist, chose the giant panda for the official WWF logo because it's recognizable, and, since it's black and white, also easy to reproduce graphically.

erners track the panda but would not kill one and were very reluctant to allow a dead specimen into their compound. After a panda had been prepared for the museum taxidermists and shipped off, the Lolo guides called in a local priest to perform a cleansing ceremony to purify the area from the shadow of the panda's death.

In 1936, soon after Su Lin, the first live panda to leave China, arrived in Chicago's Brookfield Zoo, Americans began to make up for the centuries of neglect. From the late 1930s until the present, the panda's familiar form has lent itself to everything from earmuffs to salt and pepper shakers. Porcelain figurines, plant pots, and furry stuffed toys appeared first. Then, in 1961, the World Wildlife Fund chose the panda for its logo, making it the symbol of endangered species everywhere. Since then it has not only become a rallying point for the conservation of wildlife, but synonymous with the conservation movement. When the pandas arrived at the National Zoo in Washington, D.C., the panda craze covered every-

tage, issued a set of postage stamps featuring pandas along with golden monkeys, Manchurian cranes, and others.

In its position statement on the giant panda, the American Association of Zoological Parks and Aquariums (AAZPA) summed up the panda's role well:

> In the world of wild animals, the strange and delightful giant panda is unexcelled in public interest and affection. This interest and the panda's gravely endangered status make it a particularly effective and poignant tool in the increasing educational effort to raise the public consciousness of the plight of the earth's vanishing species.

Once a symbol of the "big game hunt," the giant panda now officially represents threatened creatures all over the world—and the very fragility of the earth itself.

*chapter*

# MEET
# THE PANDA

*one*

Studies show that the panda's relatively large head, large ears, and big eyes are the features that make them so instantly lovable—especially to kids. Perhaps it is because these features remind us of a human child.

© Sharon Cummings

Nearly everyone knows what the giant panda looks like—the slightly sad half-closed eyes surrounded by black patches, the round black ears set against the white fur of its face. The panda's legs are black and the black fur of its forelegs extends in a band that covers its chest and meets at the shoulders. Its fur is thick, dense, wiry and slightly oily to protect it from the rain and cold of its mountain habitat. In short, it looks just like the plush panda in the toy store.

While the sharp contrast of black and white distinguishes the panda from other animals, those looking for pandas describe how easily the animal blends in with its surroundings when it is up in a tree. When threatened, the panda climbs a tree and sits motionless in a

fork between two branches. The panda's black areas blend into the branches and its white fur is indistinguishable from the usually cloudy sky. In the forest, the patches of black and white fade into obscurity within 25 or 30 feet (10 or 12 meters).

Although the panda's outward appearance is so clear-cut that almost any child can easily draw one, its physical structure is far more complex—so much so, in fact, that scientists have had trouble agreeing on exactly which family it belongs to. The panda has several anatomical features that both fascinate and puzzle those who study them.

Climbing trees is common bear behavior, but bears rarely sit on their hind haunches. In order to bring food to its mouth, a panda has no choice but to sit or lie down to eat—another aspect that lends it a humanlike quality. Large forearms help pandas to climb easily.

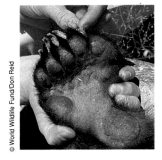

The first is the panda's peculiar thumb. The human hand has four fingers in a row and an opposable thumb—that singular mark of the primates to which so much of our advancement relative to other creatures has been credited. The panda's paw, however, has all five digits lined up together; below them, a padlike sixth digit, moved by a separate set of muscles, works in the opposite direction of the five fingers.

What are the scientific differences between human thumbs and this sixth digit of the panda's? Anatomically, the panda "thumb" isn't a finger but an elongated bone in the wrist

(Top) Note the pad covering the "thumb" on the left side of the panda's paw. (Right) Anatomical adaptations allow pandas to hold a stalk of bamboo in one paw. (Inset) In other animals the radial sesimoid bone is just one of many small bones in the wrist, but in the giant panda it has grown into a useful sixth digit.

radial sesamoid

called the *radial sesamoid*. In most carnivores, this is just one of the small bones that make up the wrist. But because it helped them to get a better grasp on the bamboo, in the panda it evolved into a much longer bone—although not as long as the five true fingers—that was able to do the work of a thumb.

The growth of the radial sesamoid alone would have been of little use to a panda trying to grip his bamboo lunch had it not been accompanied by a set of muscles to operate it. Like the sesamoid bone, these muscles did not spring from nothing; they were already existing muscles called into a new use and adapted to control the new bone. An abductor muscle pulls the panda's thumb away from the fingers, while two smaller ones work together to pull it back.

The panda's hand may be less adroit than the human hand, but it works. Between the pad of the thumb and the pad of the fingers is a trough just the right size for bamboo stalks to lie in. Pandas are able to pick up a single piece of straw and small bits of food with their forepaws, and Hsing-Hsing and Ling-Ling, at the National Zoo in Washington, D.C., can even pick up their metal food dishes by their narrow edges.

The whole arrangement, one cannot help but muse, would have delighted Charles Darwin, for it is a fine example of evolution. Don Reid explains how the forces of evolution work:

> Evolution is not a response to a need in an animal's lifestyle, as though it could occur to make a part of an animal more efficient or useful. (If it were it would have changed the panda's stomach.) Rather there is a gradual chance shift in the anatomy of some individual animals, who then have what is called a 'selective advantage' and are more fit for survival.

© Sharon Cummings/Marvin Dembinsky Photo Associates

Fortunately, the bears from which pandas descended already had slightly enlarged radial sesamoids. The two muscles that control the thumb also exist in bears and are attached in the same places. Both bears and raccoons—another of the panda's relatives—are far more adept than other carnivores at using their forearms.

Giant pandas share several anatomical features with black bear cubs that make them well suited to climbing trees. They have claws for holding on and their forelimbs are more developed than their hindlimbs. This is different than animals that run a lot, whose limb development is more symmetrical, or animals that crouch and jump, such as the lynx, whose hindlimbs are more developed than their forelimbs.

Compare the shape of this bear's head to that of the giant panda on the opposite page. The bear's is smaller, relative to its body size, and more pointed, like the muzzle of a dog. The giant panda's head is larger and rounder, due to its enlarged jaws used for crushing bamboo.

Why did this strange makeshift thumb develop as it did when there was a fifth finger already there? Why didn't *it* evolve into the thumb? The answer to this question lies farther back in time, when the carnivores had already begun to specialize. By the time the panda split off from the main trunk of its ancestral family tree, the true thumb had already been put to another use as part of a large paw needed for running and climbing. It was far too committed to these uses to be diverted to grasping bamboo.

The panda evolved and adapted in other ways as its diet became increasingly vegetarian in nature. By comparing the shape and size of a bear's head with the panda's, a significant difference becomes evident: Like its paws, the panda's head has adjusted to handling the tough, woody bamboo stems.

© Sharon Cummings

The panda's head is round, wide, and very large in comparison to the rest of the body. Its jaws are enlarged, and the typical tooth structure of the carnivore has been modified for crushing and grinding. The panda's molars are broad and heavily cusped, as are its premolars. Equipped with massive jaw muscles and powerful teeth, the panda can crush bamboo easily. In fact, a captive panda in the Wolong Reserve in China ate its aluminum feeding dish, chewing it into pieces small enough to pass through its digestive system. Desmond Morris best described the strength and design of the panda's jaw in his book *Men and Pandas* when he said, "The whole head of the panda has become modified as a crushing machine."

The eye of the panda has a vertical pupil like that of a cat, perhaps giving rise to the traditional Chinese name *daxiong mao,* which means "large bear cat."

The thickly furred panda tail neatly folds down to cover the glands that are used for scent marking. When extended the tail serves as a convenient brush for wiping the slightly acid scent onto trees.

The panda's legs are powerful, and it walks with a rolling gait, rarely running. Although the panda is able to move faster in the open, the bamboo thickets do not accommodate speedy travel. The panda's low shape and heavy, powerful shoulders are perfect for passing through dense thickets and under the fallen trees that cover the mountainsides of its homeland.

© Sharon Cummings

Pandas climb trees easily. If the tree is large in diameter and vertical, they hug the tree and alternate "steps" with fore- and hindpaws, clutching the bark with their sharp claws. The panda climbs or descends trees with even a slight angle easily by walking along them on all fours. Although pandas can stand on their two hind legs—and often do so to feed—they do not walk upright as bears are known to do.

A full-grown panda may weigh up to 300 pounds (136 kilograms) and will measure between 5 and 6 feet (1.5 to 1.8 meters) from nose to tail. Males usually weigh 10 to 20 percent more than females.

Giant pandas have a distinctive way of walking that differentiates them from bears—they're pigeon toed. Scientists have yet to discover a reason for this peculiar characteristic.

# THE PANDA'S FAMILY TREE

Until the late 1980s, there was considerable debate as to whether the panda was related more closely to the bears or to the raccoons. This battle over the panda's ancestry has raged ever since the animal's introduction to the world outside of China. Père David, the French naturalist who first brought word of pandas to the western world in 1869, classified them as a new species of bear, *Ursus melanoleucus,* or the "black and white bear." Pandas look and walk like bears, and it was logical that the genus was that of the bear.

But controversy arose when Père David sent a skeleton of one to his colleague, Alphonse Milne-Edwards, who later became director of the Museum of Natural History in Paris. Milne-Edwards decided that the panda was more closely akin to the red panda *(Ailurus fulgens),* already known to be a relative of the raccoon. The panda's

**Bears eat just about everything—plants, insects, fish, animals, ants, honey bees, berries, and nuts.**

resemblance to the bear was merely a superficial holdover from the common ancestry shared in the prehistoric past by both bears and raccoons.

Milne-Edwards renamed the panda *Ailuro-poda melanoleuca,* or the "black-and-white cat-foot." The association with cats is a familiar theme, since the red panda is also called the fire cat and the shining bearcat. Milne-Edwards classed the giant panda in the family *Procyonidae.*

This was not the last word on the subject, however. Scientists continued to be haunted by the suspicion that an animal that looked so much like a bear might indeed be one. The panda's brain, respiratory system, and ear bones are all bearlike, and, like bears, pandas walk with the pads of all four paws touching the ground.

Others argued, however, that pandas don't hibernate and have quite different teeth, more like those of the red panda, with whom they also share a bamboo diet. The shape and construction of the two species' skulls is the same, as are the main color pattern of their fur, their scent-

marking habits and voices, and much of their digestive systems. More than forty academic papers were published on the subject without any consensus, and the scientific name has changed back and forth.

In 1964, D. Dwight Davis, curator of mammals at Chicago's Field Museum of Natural History, made one of the most thorough and detailed anatomical studies of all time—the most complete study that had been made of a panda up until that time. Davis examined fifty organs, comparing them in painstaking detail to both bears and raccoons. He published his conclusions in a monograph, *The Giant Panda: A Morphological Study of Evolutionary Mechanisms*, accompanied by

(Top) The giant panda and the red panda live in the same mountain areas of China and both eat bamboo. The red panda has some of the same modifications that pandas do to help them grasp and eat bamboo stalks, including the enlargement of the radial sesimoid bone and the molars. (Lower right) Raccoons are similar in size and markings to red pandas but live only in North America.

© Lois & George Cox

© Mark Sherman/Bruce Coleman, Inc.

**The red panda, also known as the "lesser panda", is approximately 3 feet (.9 meters) long, including the tail, and weighs 10 to 15 pounds (4.5 to 6.8 kg). It climbs in trees to eat fruits such as wild cherries and mountain ash berries as well as bamboo.**

equally detailed anatomical illustrations by H. E. Givens. Together, the monograph and illustrations consider and describe the panda's nerves, bones, blood vessels, muscles, and organs. Davis concluded that "every morphological feature examined indicates that the giant panda is nothing more than a highly specialized bear."

Not only did Davis present detailed physical evidence, but he offered an explanation, based on his observations, of how and why this relative of the bear exhibited so many features common to the red panda. It had been, after all, the red panda that was the stumbling block right along. Had it not existed—seemingly the link between the panda and the raccoon—most likely the panda's heritage would never have been in question.

The key to Davis's conclusion was the assertion that the similarities between the giant and red pandas were evolutionary. They were two different, distantly related carnivores that had adapted to similar environments and diets in much the same ways. Their similarities, Davis said, resulted "from similar function requirements, not from common ancestry."

Other totally unrelated creatures have developed similar features. The whale developed a tail like a fish when it moved from the land to a sea environment, but this does not indicate that whales are related to fish.

Davis was able to demonstrate how and why the panda had changed: It had shifted from eating a diet composed primarily of meat to an almost steady diet of bamboo. Over time the panda's structure adapted into one that could handle, chew, and digest these tough plants. This adaptation accounts for the dental structure, heavy jaws, large head, heavier forelegs (to carry the additional frontal weight), and the peculiar thumb. Each one of these changes required others to balance it and, Davis concluded, the long list of panda–bear differences could have been accomplished in only six basic changes, each readily identifiable.

Such a thorough and learned study and report as D. Dwight Davis's might have ended the matter, but it didn't. Very shortly after Davis's paper was

Scientists have debated over the panda's ancestry for more than a century. The strongest evidence that they are most closely related to bears was found in their DNA structure and certain anatomical features.

published, Desmond Morris of the Zoological Society of London concluded his own study—with the finding that the pandas belonged in the raccoon family. Morris's conclusion was corroborated by other similar but independent findings at the University of Ghana.

In 1983, Stephen O'Brien and his colleagues at the National Cancer Institute were asked to investigate the paternity of the cub born to Ling-Ling at the National Zoo in Washington, D.C. Since Ling-Ling had mated with Hsing-Hsing, the zoo's male panda, and had also been artificially inseminated with semen from London's Chia-Chia, zoo officials were anxious to know which of these had resulted in her pregnancy.

Although Ling-Ling's cub had died, paternity could be determined by a method called *gel electrophoresis*, which analyzes proteins from tissue samples. While they were doing this analysis, the scientists decided to use the same techniques to investigate the bear–raccoon question. They used proteins from the giant panda, the red panda, the raccoon, and a number of different bears. The

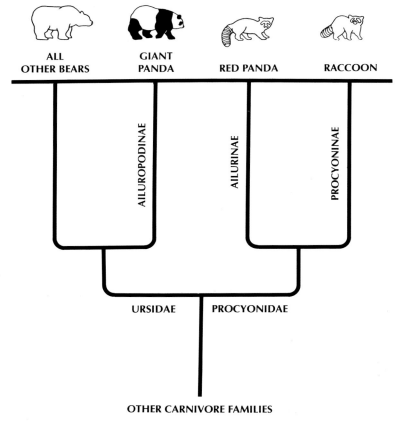

ALL OTHER BEARS     GIANT PANDA     RED PANDA     RACCOON

AILUROPODINAE     AILURINAE     PROCYONINAE

URSIDAE     PROCYONIDAE

OTHER CARNIVORE FAMILIES

© Steve Arcella

Though giant pandas are now generally believed to be a part of the bear family, one alternative hypothesis suggests they are descended from the red panda. Giant panda expert Don Reid explains: "The red panda is energetically right on the edge in its mountainous home because it is very difficult for it to gain enough nutrients from bamboo. If it had a larger body—in other words a smaller surface area to volume ratio—it would loose heat less quickly, and would therefore be less stressed energetically. For this reason, there is a strong selective force for red pandas to be larger, which could indicate that the giant panda evolved from the red panda."

DNA sequences of the panda would be most like those of its closest relative.

A series of four independent tests led these scientists on a genetic treasure hunt. They approached the question of the panda's ancestry from several directions, comparing the overall binding of the genetic structures, the similarities of specific genes, the reactions of the various immune systems to tissues of the others, and the number and forms of chromosomes.

The molecular findings confirmed what D. Dwight Davis had discovered by studying the panda's anatomy; that red pandas and raccoons share one pattern, while giant pandas and bears have a much different arrangement. The researchers' curiosity was then aroused about when this genetic divergence occurred. They knew who was related to whom, but not when it happened.

The National Cancer Institute scientists chose to place the panda on the evolutionary timetable by comparing it to a different group of carnivores whose history was known. Stephen O'Brien describes this process in his article, "The Ancestry of the Giant Panda" in the November 1987 issue of *Scientific American:* "If we could show that two species of primates had the same molecular distance values as two species of bears, we could assume that both groups diverged about the same time."

By repeating the same tests on a group of different primates and comparing the results to their panda studies, the scientists estimated that the raccoons split off from the bear lineage between thirty and fifty million years ago. The pandas diverged from the bears about ten million years later.

It had taken well over a century for science to generally accept what Père David had observed and what children all over the world already knew: that the panda was a very special bear.

# THE PANDA AT HOME IN THE WILD

During all this time the panda lived its quiet life deep in the forests of the mist-shrouded mountains of Szechwan, Gansu, and Shaanxi, quite unaware of the excitement it was causing. The same vegetarian diet that had created the changes that so perplexed scientists was the greatest of the panda's ongoing concerns. While zoologists worried about genetics, the panda searched for bamboo.

The panda's home is in the rugged terrain of the mountains of southwestern China, which rise tier after tier to the Tibetan Plateau at elevations of 5000 to 10,000 feet (1,969 to 3,937 meters). The Tibetans call this land the Ngam-grog-chi—the land of deep corrugations. The sharp peaks are frequently lost in the clouds that cover the area, providing the constant moisture bamboo thrives on. Even though the forest is cold and snow-covered in winter, it is still quite green with fir and hemlock and entire forests of gnarled and twisted rhododendrons—more than one hundred varieties of them. In the summer, temperatures rarely rise above 50°F. (10° C.) and rain is almost continuous.

The panda's range was once much wider than this small corner of China. Fossil records of three million years ago show that it lived as far north as Beijing (Peking), south to Hong Kong and east along the south banks of the Yangtze River almost to Shanghai. Its range extended well into Burma.

Arrow bamboo grows almost year round in the subalpine fir and birch forest in Wolong Reserve.

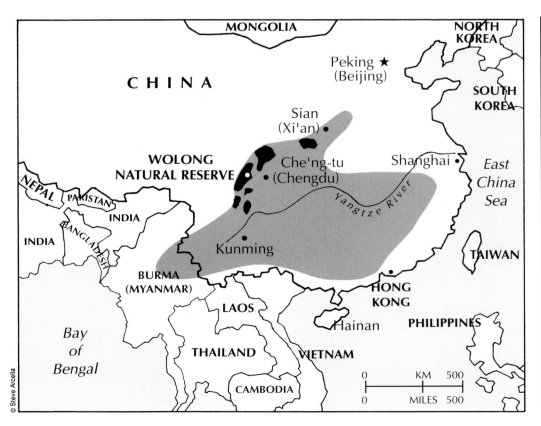

∎ **Pandas Today**

▨ **Known Prehistoric Range of Pandas**

As farms spread up steep valley sides, much of the forested panda habitat is removed at lower elevations, leaving only isolated patches on ridge tops. Note the outline of fields in this winter photo. Subsistence agriculture is an arduous life for the people who share the mountain regions with the panda as well.

Historical records of the panda exist from the first two centuries A.D. as far north as Sian and in the eastern mountains not far from the East China Sea. As late as the mid-1800s it was recorded in the mountains halfway between Che'ng-tu and the coast.

But the bamboo forest and its canopy of larger trees that once covered vast areas of China have largely been destroyed for timber, potash, and charcoal, and to clear land for farming. At the same time that this has limited the panda's range, poaching has decreased its numbers.

The narrowing of the panda's habitat has not been a sudden phenomenon but a steady encroachment. William Sheldon, an explorer who wrote on agriculture in the 1930s, says: "Even at two thousand feet above the river bottom, on a slope so steep that you looked down over cliffs at a sixty degree angle to the stream below, every possible acre of earth seemed planted with corn." Even deeper into the mountains, he laments, "the complete denudation of the trees in the more settled sections at lower altitudes has been very depressing."

© Okapia/Photo Researchers, Inc.

Fortunately for the panda, it has few enemies in nature. Adult pandas are much larger than the predators who live in its territory, and are able to protect themselves and their young with claws and strong jaws. Weasels, martens, and golden cats may attack unguarded cubs, and wild dogs and leopards may kill old or sick adults, but predation is not a serious concern.

The panda is a solitary animal in its wild home and meets other pandas only briefly except during mating season. Most pandas' ranges are small—between 1¹⁄₂ to 2¹⁄₂ square miles (3.8 to 6.5 square kilometers)—and may overlap with the range of other pandas. Within these overlapping areas each female has a home ground of about 100 acres (40.5 hectares) that is exclusively her own. Males sometimes share the same range, but they generally avoid each other's company. When pandas do meet, they are hardly sociable and are very noisy. Encounters are marked with a series of barks, bleats, yips, and squeals.

Pandas seem to be able to avoid confrontations fairly easily through scent marking. By rubbing their brushlike tails against a tree and depositing on it the secretions of their scent glands, pandas identify the area and also tell other pandas how long ago they were there, whether they are male or female, and if they are ready to mate.

(Above) Due to the dense bamboo, observing and photographing pandas in the wild is chancy at best.
(Left) Pandas in the wild seem to be chewing on stems of bamboo almost constantly.

# THE PANDA'S NEIGHBORS

*Asiatic Black Bear:* A bear about the same size as the giant panda that eats vegetables, berries, and acorns.

*Golden monkey:* A large snub-nosed monkey with a blue face and a silky mane of golden hair that may be twelve to eighteen inches (3 to 4.5 decimeters) long. Rare and found only in this area of China, these animals travel in bands of seventy or so in the winter and more than three hundred in the summer.

*Takin:* A furry, chunky goat antelope called the wild cow locally. The takin has short, thick legs, a humped back, a large nose, and swept-back horns. It moves with agility on the cliffs and through the bamboo. Like the panda, the takin is an endangered species protected in the Wolong Reserve. The takin of this area is golden in color.

*Goral:* A small antelope with short horns that lives among the cliffs of the river gorges between 2,500 and 10,000 feet (762 and 3,048 meters).

*Musk deer:* A small deer 3 feet (1 meter) tall that weighs less than 42 pounds (19 kilograms) and has short horns hidden in its fur. It lives in the bamboo regions and is poached by the thousands each year for its egg-size scent gland used in perfume making.

*Leopard:* The spotted variety preys on baby pandas and on older, infirm adults.

*Serow:* A common, smaller, surefooted goat antelope with short horns. It weighs 200 to 250 pounds, (90 to 113 kilograms), about one third the weight of a takin. The serow is very dark, but some specimens have white manes.

*Wild boar:* A plentiful animal from the Szechwan Plain to the highest edge of the bamboo forests.

*Muntjac:* A barking deer with short horns that lives among the bamboo and raids farmer's cornfields.

*Tufted deer:* A short-horned deer that rarely leaves the woods and defends itself with sharp canine teeth.

(Above) Pandas use their molars, not their incisors, to bite off pieces of bamboo. (Right) Umbrella bamboo, the preferred spring food of pandas in Wolong, grows to over 9 feet high (2.7 meters) in only six weeks. (Far right) Lying down is another way pandas free up their forepaws for feeding.

# FEEDING IN THE WILD

The panda's life revolves around bamboo. Its habitat is determined by where the bamboo grows, and most of its waking hours are spent eating. Although the panda will eat crocus, iris, an occasional small bamboo rat or bird, and will invade a farmer's cornfield or beehive (the panda has a sweet tooth), its principal food consists of stems, twigs, leaves, and young shoots of bamboo. The leaves and tender stems are its favorite part.

Fortunately, bamboo grows quickly, since a single panda can consume over 40 pounds (18 kilograms), or several hundred stalks each day. When its diet is of new shoots—much higher in water content—a panda can consume 85 pounds (39 kilograms) in a single day.

Since the panda spends some twelve to fourteen hours each day eating, it usually chooses a comfortable position lying on its back or side, or sitting in a relaxed slouch. With paws and teeth working together, the panda will occasionally strip off the tough outer coating of the bamboo to reach the juicy center. If the shoot is long, the panda may bite it in half and eat each piece end

© Sharon Cummings

first like a pencil sharpener gone wild, or the panda may chew along it as though playing a flute.

Because of its "thumb," the panda can pick up even small stems of bamboo and put them in its mouth or reach up and pull down pliable stems to munch on instead of eating off the ground or only from bushes within reach of their mouths, as less dexterous animals must.

George Schaller, of the New York Zoological Society, who has spent more time observing pandas in the wild than any other Westerner, recorded that a panda he was following ate portions of 3,481 different stems of bamboo in one day.

Giant pandas in the wild eat bamboo year round, but which part of the plant they choose shifts with the seasons. Panda expert Don Reid explains: "Apart from eating the tender young shoots when they come up the animals have a choice of eating the stems or the leaves. The leaves are generally preferred because they have a higher nutritional content. The stem is less nutritious, and because it's so fibrous, it's also harder to chew and harder to swallow. The shift between leaves and stems also appears to be related to the loss of leaves with the frost in the autumn. All bamboos maintain some of their green leaves and living stems throughout the winter—and that allows the panda to go through winter without hibernating."

© World Wildlife Fund/Don Reid

Although the paws, jaws, and teeth of this carnivore have adapted to eating bamboo, the panda's digestive system is still essentially that of a meat eater. The panda's stomach walls have become very tough and muscular, but the intestine is still short like that of the classic carnivore—less than 30 feet (9 meters) long, or five times its body length. Most herbivores have long intestines to help them absorb more of the nutrients from a plant diet; the long intestines of cattle are over twenty times their body length. More importantly, the panda does not have the typical herbivore's multi-compartmental stomach and as a consequence utilizes very little of the food it ingests, absorbing less than 20 percent of the bamboo's potential nutrients and leaving a good deal undigested. (This compares with as much as 80 percent efficiency in some herbivores.) These factors, of course, explain the panda's voracious appetite. Since it draws scant nutrition from each piece, it must eat more.

On the other hand, the panda's specialized and restricted diet offers certain advantages. The panda is virtually alone in its diet, with almost no competition for the ample supply of bamboo that covers the mountains. Bamboo is available year round, even in the winter, so there is no need for the panda to hibernate, to hoard food for winter, or to migrate seasonally for a food supply. (Pandas do migrate on a limited basis, moving in the spring from their regular large stands of arrow bamboo and other high-altitude varieties to the lower slopes for a taste of the tender shoots of umbrella bamboo.)

The panda's thirst is legendary among the local peoples. Many people claim to have seen pandas

Don Reid explains a common ecological story in the panda's habitat: "The bamboo undergrowth in the forest is out competing most tree seedlings that happen to germinate. So the best way those seedlings can take over for their parents and regenerate the canopy is if they happen to land and take hold on a fallen log where they're above the bamboo, or, if there is some disturbance—such as a strong wind storm—whereby the adult trees fall over and the soil is exposed. Then you get a little window in time that allows the trees to take hold before the bamboo. A bigger window occurs when the bamboo naturally flowers and dies, giving tree seedlings at least a five year head start on the slower growing bamboo seedlings. Old forest growth produces the hollow fir trees pandas use for maternal dens, which are quite rare and getting rarer as forest is removed from their habitat."

drink so much water that they fall over, unable to move for several hours—but this is unconfirmed by any scientific observation. The panda does, however, drink prodigious amounts from the cold mountain streams that plummet down the steep ravines. One legend claims that the panda drinks in an effort to quiet the rushing torrents whose roar disturbs its sleep.

With twelve to fourteen hours of each day spent browsing and eating, mostly in the hours sur-rounding dawn and dusk, the panda spends much of the rest of its time sleeping, usually two to four hours at a time.

George Schaller describes following a panda on its feeding rounds, watching it eat and then lie down in the snow wherever it happened to be, using a log as a backrest. The panda's fur is so dense that it provides abundant insulation with-out the panda having to search for a protective den before sleeping.

© Ken Johnson

(Far left) Arrow bamboo at high elevations is sparse but still ubiquitous. Pandas feed in this zone only when the richer growth at lower elevations is lost— such as after a bamboo flowering. (Left) While tracking Zhen-Zhen, a study animal in the wild, Ken Johnson, a field biologist and panda expert, observed a dramatic shift in her mood—she became irritable like a child in need of a nap. (Bottom) After the above photo was taken, she stalked off through the bamboo, curled up into a ball, and almost immediately began snoring.

# EARLY VIEWS OF THE PANDA'S HOME

*A frightening region of deep and craggy mountains, heaped up one upon the other—the beginning of the high Tibetan plateau. Peaks of perpetual snow raise themselves not far from here.*

*—Père Armand David, March 21, 1869*

*A lonely, wild and unutterably beautiful place with an impetuous stream that dashed down a rocky bed below. At the right of us a sheer cliff rose steeply and then blended with the mountain; the stream flung itself on the rocky base and then disappeared through a rocky defile. The far end of the valley lost itself in an ever-rising range. . . . The hills were flaming with autumn color—crimson, orange and russet. Little groves of aspen in the valley rustled dryly in the gentle wind and sunshine on the aquamarine waters of the Tsaopo-go turned every small ripple into sparkling clusters of jewels.*
—Ruth Harkness in *The Lady and the Panda, 1936.*

*The valley was filled with mist, the sun was up and shining brilliantly on the peaks of the mountains west of us. Clouds would often obliterate the slopes while the summits pierced the heavens above, or drifting higher, banners of mist would cling to the peaks alone. At no one moment was the view entirely clear. The green of the slopes and jagged irregular array of peaks, precipitous cliffs, rhododendrons, and spruces leading down to the invisible abysses of the valleys below were visible at different times....We had hardly had an opportunity to survey the slopes with our binoculars before a sea of fog fairly boiled up from the valley bottom, completely obscuring the nearest peak.*
—William Sheldon, in *The Wilderness Home of the Giant Panda*, 1934

*"[In the spring] the mountainsides were glorious with rhododendrons, varying in hue from deep purple to white. Pink was the prevailing color. In places the ground was sprinkled with a small blue member of the orchid family. Blue lilies, forget-me-nots, primroses, and a diminutive yellow flower dotted the pathside."*

—Kermit Roosevelt in *Trailing the Giant Panda*, 1929

# MATING AND PANDA CUBS

The mating habits of pandas in the wild are difficult for scientists to observe. The first and obvious question is how animals whose lives are so solitary find each other when it is time to mate. Solving this problem, along with delineation of territories, is the purpose of scent marking. In addition, pandas—normally very quiet animals—become quite vocal when they are ready to mate, usually in late March and April.

George Schaller of the New York Zoological Society is one of the few people who has observed the panda mating ritual. It happened when he was using a radio to monitor a collared female panda in the Wolong Reserve. Schaller describes it in his December 1981 *National Geographic* magazine article "Pandas in the Wild."

Zhen-Zhen is restless, according to our radio signals. Listening from a nearby ridge, we can hear a male emitting the whines and barks that are the equivalent of a panda love song. The next day I observe the pair and soon see a smaller male arrive. The larger male, threatening and charging, soon drives him away from the female.

I stand near a large fir tree and shortly Zhen-Zhen comes panting up the trail. Unalarmed, she goes to the other side of the tree and sits down. Soon the male comes puffing up the slope, and I back off. He simply steps over my tape recorder and follows her. I observe him mount her forty-eight times in three hours.

Schaller adds that as the three-to-five-month gestation period draws short, he and his research team will avoid Zhen-Zhen's maternity den. Because scientists in the wild are so cautious about the safety of scarce newborn pandas, they dare not risk disturbing a new mother. As a result, most of what we know about pandas' births and parenthood is from observation in zoos.

The newborn panda is pink, almost completely furless, and about the size of a quarter-pound stick of butter. Its eyes remain closed for a month after birth. Because the length of the gestation period is so variable and because the baby panda is so underdeveloped (the baby pandas are born at a stage of development that should be reached

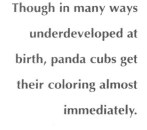

Though in many ways underdeveloped at birth, panda cubs get their coloring almost immediately.

© World Wildlife Fund for Nature/Peking Zoological Garden

at about six weeks of gestation in an animal of the panda's size) researchers think that the fertilized egg is not implanted immediately but floats in the uterus for as long as four months before being implanted and developing into an infant.

Since the newborn panda is so completely help-less and dependent on the mother for the first several months, it would be virtually impossible for a mother to carry and care for two. So, although two cubs are frequently born together, the mother cares only for the stronger cub, abandoning the weaker.

For the first month, until the young panda's eyes are open and the coat of warm fur is fully grown, the mother holds the infant constantly in her furry paw. When she walks, she carries it in her mouth, and she sleeps sitting up, with the cub in her arms. Even after the first month, she only places the cub in the nest for short periods—until, at over two months old, it is able to stand up. During these brief moments the mother panda eats, but never far from the nest, most often located in a site where the bamboo is dense enough to provide food as well as cover.

During the first three months the cub can move only by rolling from side to side or by squirming,

© World Wildlife Fund/Don Reid

(Above) A mother and baby at the Beijing Zoo. Panda mothers lavish their babies with con-tinuous tender loving care until they are more than a year old. (Left) The maternal den tree used by Zhen-Zhen, a study animal in the Wolong Reserve.

© CPS/PPS/Photo Researchers, Inc.

usually lying on its back and kicking all four legs, and sleeps on its back with its front legs folded over its chest.

When the panda cub finally learns to stand, its short legs are hardly big enough to keep its round, fat stomach off the ground. Some time is required for the cub to develop the necessary coordination to be able to move all four legs in the proper sequence to walk. During this time, the cub also practices climbing, usually all over its mother. At three months, the cub weighs about 12 pounds (5.5 kilograms).

As the cub gets stronger, the mother plays with it and cuddles it and is very solicitous of its comfort. Perhaps the only part of the tiny cub that is well developed at birth is its vocal cords. For such a tiny being, the baby panda has a surprisingly loud, piercing voice, and it squawks insistently whenever it is uncomfortable. The mother panda responds with understandable speed by changing its position.

The characteristic black-and-white markings appear quickly, with eye patches visible on the cub about a week following birth. Then the ear, shoulder, and leg colorings appear.

By the time the panda is five months old, which usually coincides with the depths of winter, it has developed enough coordination to trot about and

© World Wildlife Fund/Don Reid

(Above) Panda cubs don't open their eyes until they are about one month old.

(Left) Young pandas climb trees to avoid danger.

(Far left top and bottom) A zoo employee stands by while a young panda at the Beijing Zoo tries out his climbing skills.

**Lan Tian, a baby panda born in the Wolong Reserve Breeding Facility.**

begin to eat the bamboo that will comprise its diet for the rest of its life. The baby panda will continue to nurse until it is eight or nine months old and will remain dependent on its mother until it is approximately a year and a half old.

The panda's disposition is well-suited to parenting. Neither males nor females are highly excitable. Except during mating season, fighting is almost unknown, and even then such behavior is characterized more by charging and growling rather than by physical contact. The mother panda can be very aggressive, however, in protecting her cub from predators. Pandas in the wild, researchers have observed, have placid, easy going natures, and although they spend most of their lives in solitary seclusion, the females respond well to the exacting requirements of motherhood. Considering the many problems that beset panda reproduction in the wild, this is most fortunate.

# WHAT WE KNOW AND HOW WE'VE LEARNED IT

The previous discussion of pandas in the wild has referred to the writings of those few people who have been able to observe them in their native habitat. Père David; Teddy and Kermit Roosevelt; William Sheldon; the Canadian biologist, Don Reid; Ken Johnson at the University of Tennessee; and George Schaller of the New York Zoological Society have each given the world a glimpse of the panda's life in the mountains of China.

George Schaller, with his coworkers Hu Jinchu, Pan Wenshi, and Zhou Jing, spent over four years at the Wolong Reserve studying pandas with the most up-to-date scientific equipment. Their book, *The Giant Pandas of Wolong*, brought invaluable information to the scentific community, and Schaller's *National Geographic* articles have brought their firsthand observations to popular attention. While on a collecting expedition for a museum, Sheldon also documented his observations of other animals, in the panda's habitat. (See "The Pandas' Neighbors," p. 32.) How these naturalists and scientists work is interesting in itself.

The first thing each of these scientists speaks of is the great difficulty involved in observing pandas. Weather, altitude, and terrain all seem to conspire against their work. Couple these factors with the reclusive nature of the pandas and their ability to remain invisible in the bamboo thickets, and it's easy to see why the slim chance of seeing even one panda has haunted every researcher who made an attempt.

Père David's description in his diary calls up images of the difficult terrain that later writers could only echo:

> We pull ourselves up from rock to rock by clinging to trees and roots. All that is not vertical is covered with frozen snow. . . . After we have reached a certain height it becomes impossible to ascend without slipping and falling on the ice. We are badly scratched and our clothing and equipment is soaked. . . . Sometimes we are plunged into the half-melted snow, or the trees which we clutch and break, and we roll to another tree or nearby rock.

Sixty years later, Kermit Roosevelt takes up the narrative in *Trailing the Giant Panda:*

> The fallen logs were slippery with snow and ice. Here we could crawl through and under; there we had to crawl laboriously around and over. The bamboo jungle proved a particularly unpleasant form of obstacle course, where many of the feathery tops were weighed down by snow and frozen fast in the ground. Drenched by rain and soaked by snow, whenever a moment's halt was called we alternately shivered and panted.

Scientists have spent months in the panda's habitat without seeing a single animal. Because a person in the bamboo makes so much noise, it is nearly impossible to observe the animal's behavior without bias.

At high altitudes, the heat of the sun will melt the snow on these slopes within a day—making the mountains in the panda's habitat very wet and slippery.

William Sheldon found that the only way to get through the bamboo's dense growth was to bend double or crawl on his hands and knees. Dean Sage, leader of Sheldon's expedition and an avid sportsman with extensive experience in Alaska and Africa, described trying to cut across a slope between two ridges:

Leaving the trail, we plunged into the wet bamboos and entered upon the toughest piece of going I have ever run up against. Clinging precariously to a precipitous grade we literally clawed our way inch by inch through a tangled mass of bamboos, thorns, trailing vines and creepers that caught hold of our feet, our rifles, and in short, everything that could be caught hold of and tripped or snarled up. The bamboos grew only a few inches apart, and they grew in every direction but upside down, so that we had to alternately push them apart to crawl under them or climb over them.... Cliffs and ledges covered with treacherous loose moss, where a slip would mean a dangerous fall, did not add to the security of our progress.

Scientists who track pandas in the wild are severely hindered by the more robust species of bamboo. "It is like going through a maze," says biologist Don Reid, "or like trying to climb through the bars of a prison window."

Don Reid explains what a field biologist would look for in the feeding site shown below: "First, there are two droppings. What the droppings show is that the bamboo is incredibly poorly digested. By measuring the length of the bite size pieces of bamboo you can determine the width between the animal's molars, and with this measurement, determine which of three age classes it belongs in—juvenile, subadult, or adult.

"There are also several stumps of bamboo, as well as the discarded leafy tops of stems. Though pandas prefer leaves to stems, late in the year there are not enough leaves for them to bother with and they will discard them immediately. By doing intricate measurements of the stumps and the tops—and then measuring the other stalks in the general vicinity that haven't been touched—we can determine approximately how much has been eaten. Then, by trailing an animal for twenty-four hours, we can begin to get a picture of what they're eating in a day, and, based on what is left undigested in droppings, what the nutritional benefit has been."

(Right) Researchers gain two kinds of information from radio collars—the animal's location, which is plotted daily on a detailed map, and its activity patterns.

George Schaller speaks of his clothing being sodden as he followed a panda and of the 19°F. (−7C.) weather when beads of ice covered the inside walls of the tent in which he slept.

Schaller's team began a systematic program of radio collaring so that they could monitor the pandas' movements. With a radio receiver tuned to the frequency of the transmitter on the panda's collar, researchers found that they could follow and watch pandas up close or record their eating, sleeping, and travel activities from afar. The radio collars emit beeps at short intervals when pandas are moving and beep more slowly and farther apart when they sleep. The distance a panda travels in a day, researchers found, is sometimes as short as two city blocks.

To catch the pandas for collaring, Schaller's team used log traps baited with goat meat. Still carnivorous when they encounter meat, pandas

enter the log trap and a door slides down. Captured animals are tranquilized, examined, suspended upside down, and weighed on a hanging scale affixed to a pole, then fitted with radio collars. Pandas that are not full-grown are a bit of a problem, since the collar must allow room for growth but must not be loose enough to catch on limbs and trap the wearer. Fortunately, pandas don't seem to mind wearing the collars.

But even with radio to help them locate pandas, poor visibility in the bamboo thickets combine with the panda's reclusive habits to make actual sightings rare. Schaller reports that with daily excursions in a 16-square-mile (41-square-kilometer) area through which as many as eighteen pandas were known to pass, he saw only one panda a month on average.

By observing half-eaten bamboo stems, scientists can tell what kinds of bamboo a certain panda favors, how much it eats, and what sort of area it chooses to feed in. Using this method,

researchers have learned that pandas prefer an area with about 70 percent forest canopy; very important information if they are to attempt to establish and preserve panda habitats.

Droppings (which the panda leaves at a prodigious rate) contain other valuable information, and are part of the data collected to help estimate populations. Not only do they indicate what the panda has eaten, but observers can tell the age and size of a panda by measuring the length of pieces of undigested bamboo stems. The average length of the pieces reflects the width of the jaw.

In captivity, it is much easier to observe and record the panda's growth and behavior, but information obtained in this way is not always helpful in planning effective programs for protecting wild populations. Pandas' behavior in zoos is often quite different, and field study, difficult as it is, remains the only sure way to learn about the wild panda.

*chapter*

# EAST MEETS WEST AND WEST MEETS PANDAS

*two*

*P*andas were known for many centuries in China before the outside world learned of them, but even in China they were not commonly known.

The earliest mention of pandas is in *The Tribute of Yu,* which records that the emperor Yu received them more than four thousand years ago as tribute from the people of Liangchow, located about 200 miles north of the panda's present range. But the reference to the panda is by its old name, and historians are not sure whether the reference is to the giant or the red panda.

*Chi King,* the sacred book of songs, records that in 1050 B.C. the first member of the Zhou dynasty built a "park of learning" where later rulers kept live giant pandas. *The Classics of Seas and Mountains,* a geography book dating to 500 B.C., tells about the *mo* (an old name confirmed in other accounts), "a bearlike black-and-white animal that eats copper and iron," living in the Qionglai Mountains south of the Yangdao country. This description is not so farfetched when we consider that the panda's rare visits to villages were often to lick the remains of dinner out of cooking pots, which, as the natives told Ruth Harkness, the first Western explorer to bring a live panda back to the United States, the panda then "ate"—or at least chewed to pieces in its search for the last drop.

Kermit and Theodore Roosevelt procured "the skin of a rare giant panda" on a hunting trip in China in 1926. This drawing accompanied a news bulletin describing their adventures.

That pandas have always been rare—and thus a valued and treasured possession—is borne out by records of emperors giving them to respected guests and by the discovery of a panda skull in the tomb of an empress buried about 200 B.C.

The first foreigner to keep pandas may have been the tenno of Japan, to whom a Chinese emperor sent two live animals, and the pelts of seventy more, in A.D. 685. By the 1600s the peoples of western Szechwan were paying tribute to their princes in panda skins. Although no reports of the panda were recorded in Europe until the mid 1800s, it is likely that travelers on the Silk Road at least would have heard of the animals or seen a pelt.

Abbé Armand David, known more simply as Père David, was a talented Basque naturalist who had taken his holy orders in 1851 with the Mission of St. Vincent de Paul at the age of twenty-five. After a time in Italy, his superiors sent him to China, where his work as a naturalist was sponsored by the Paris Museum of Natural History.

During his twelve years in China, Père David proved an exceptionally resourceful collector of both specimens and data, sending quantities of both back to the museum. As a result, plant species and an unusual deer were named after him.

Père David had heard about a rare deer, the only remaining herd of which was kept behind

© World Wildlife Fund/Don Reid

European scientists considered giant pandas a myth, until a French Lazarist priest and explorer, Pere Armand David, saw a panda skin in 1869. Word spread, and soon pandas were sought by zoologists and big-game hunters around the world. Still, sixty years passed before a Western explorer actually saw a panda in the wild.

the high walls of the Imperial Hunting Park where no Westerners and few Chinese were allowed to enter. The good priest circled the walls frequently on his morning walks until one day he found a large pile of sand left by workmen.

Père David promptly climbed the sand pile and looked into the park, observing the deer in some detail. He later bribed a park guard and obtained a deer hide and bones to send to the museum. Sometime later he was legally able to obtain some live specimens, which were then bred successfully in European zoos.

Some years afterward, the royal herd escaped the Imperial Hunting Park after a flood damaged a wall, and were killed by peasants. The last one died in 1920 in a Peking Zoo. The progeny of the specimens Père David had sent to Paris meanwhile had thrived so that several European zoos had herds of the deer.

During his years in China, Père David made three extensive collecting trips into the hinterlands. The second of these trips was to Szechwan. On March 11, 1869, only a few days after his arrival there, Père David recorded in his diary that he had seen the "skin of the famous black and white bear" at the home of a local dignitary. Only twelve days later he noted in his diary, "My Christian hunters returned today after a ten days' absence. They bring me a young white bear, which they took alive, but unfortunately killed so it could be carried more easily." He recorded a few days later that the hunters had brought in the remains of an adult.

The puzzling question about Père David's diary is that, although no European had previously written of seeing or even hearing about the giant panda, the priest speaks of them as though their existence were already well known, calling them famous and registering no surprise at seeing their skins. He also seems to have been prepared to send out a hunting party to look for the animals within three days of his arrival.

Père David's casual references and the evident ease with which he obtained specimens indicate that the existence of pandas was common knowledge at least in Muping which is about 100 miles (62 kilometers) from Che'ng-tu, where the mission was, and that he knew of their existence before his arrival. It is quite likely that the panda was known, at least by reputation, to the missionaries of his order, which was already well established in China, long before there was any written record of them in the West.

Although Père David's panda made quite a stir in scientific circles, it did not prompt expeditions to obtain specimens for the cabinets of other museums. It was almost thirty years before a Russian explorer reported seeing panda skins and took several home. Then, in 1896, reports circulated about a group of Western hunters who had killed a panda. Of the explorers, botanists, and missionaries who worked in the area during the early years of the twentieth century, only one reported seeing a panda, although not clearly and at quite a distance.

Nearly fifty years after Père David, the first confirmed report of a Westerner seeing a live panda was by Hugo Weigold, a German zoologist who bought a live baby panda from locals. But Weigold's panda was still nursing, and with proper food unavailable, it died two days later. After sixty years of exploration, still no Westerner had seen a live panda in the wild.

The challenge was too tempting for the intrepid sons of Theodore Roosevelt to resist. Kermit and Theodore, Jr., sponsored by Chicago's Field Museum of Natural History, set out for China in 1928. They began by enlisting the help of the Lolo, the local mountain people whose reputation was as fierce as their mountain terrain. Although the Lolo did not kill pandas—and were prevented from doing so by local religious beliefs—they were not reluctant to help foreign hunters, at least not those who approached them with care and respect for local customs.

The Roosevelt party was frequently surprised by the lack of communication throughout western China. The magistrate of a town not 25 miles (40 kilometers) from the center of

panda country who had been born and raised there had never heard of pandas. However, the Roosevelts already knew that the panda was elusive and were not surprised to hear that very few of the hunters they employed had ever seen one alive.

The brothers and their party combed the bamboo forests from early February until mid-April before securing a specimen—the first and only panda they saw on the expedition. It was the Roosevelt brothers who first observed that the panda lived in isolated pockets, not one contiguous territory.

The Roosevelts returned home with the first giant panda ever displayed in an American museum, setting off a series of expeditions by other museums. Of these, only the Dean Sage expedition for the American Museum of Natural History in New York during 1934–35 also included a detailed scientific study of the area and of the habits of the panda and other wildlife. Sage's study remained the only one for many years, with his field notes, diaries, articles, and eventually a book, *The Wilderness Home of the Giant Panda*, the only source of information about pandas in the wild.

Although to our modern, conservation-minded way of thinking, the shooting of such a rare animal—even for scientific study and museum exhibit—is regrettable, one cannot help

New York Public Library Picture Collection

**An early stuffed panda exhibited at the British Museum of Natural History.**

but admire these early hunter-explorers. The conditions of their travel in China made the rigors of the African bush seem almost tame. The discomforts were great and the dangers real and omnipresent; stories of bad trails, bandits, and precarious bridges are recurring themes in all their accounts. Theodore Roosevelt, Jr., wrote:

Our path led over the flimsiest of branch platforms skirting a sheer cliff with rapids fifty feet below. It is said that these are never repaired unless someone breaks through and falls into the stream.

The very few explorers who succeeded in shooting a specimen made no dent in the panda population and actually may have saved the panda by bringing it to public attention in time to save at least part of its habitat. The accounts of these early adventurers led to another kind of hunter—and certainly to the most unlikely explorer to brave the panda's homeland.

New York Public Library Picture Collection

## BRING 'EM BACK ALIVE

Ruth Harkness was a New York dress designer. When she married William Harkness in 1934, he had recently returned from the island of Komodo with three giant dragon lizards he had captured live for the New York Zoological Society. The Roosevelt brothers' book, *Trailing the Giant Panda*, had fired William Harkness's imagination, and he was determined to bring back a live panda to the United States. He was in the process of mounting an expedition into Szechwan at the time he and Ruth married.

Two weeks later he left for China, and Ruth stayed in New York. "Women are a handicap on a man's expedition," she was told, and it was true

that she had no experience with field conditions. A year and a half later, after sporadic news of delays in getting a permit to travel into the interior, she received word that William had died in Shanghai.

Over the objections of nearly everyone, Ruth decided to carry on the expedition. Everything was in place for her—the people, the equipment, and the contacts, but she knew almost nothing about China and even less about pandas. Even so, Ruth Harkness set out on her highly unlikely adventure.

Like the scientists and hunters before her, Ruth found that the local people knew very little about the panda. It was the animal, she was told, that came when they were out of the village and chewed up their cooking pots (the panda's habits had evidently changed very little since 500 B.C., when they were recorded to have done the same

Explorer William Harkness. After his death while on an expedition to capture a giant panda, his wife Ruth travelled to China and returned with Su Lin, the first live panda to reach the United States.

Since Su Lin's arrival in 1936, giant pandas have become star attractions at American zoos. Hsing-Hsing and Ling-Ling living at the National Zoo in Washington D.C. are perhaps the most famous panda couple of all.

thing). But from the descriptions she was given of its looks, it became clear that almost no one had seen one. "Some said it was white with black markings—some said it was black with white stripes. Depending on the speaker, it was as big as a horse or as small as a dog."

Ruth hired the brother of the Roosevelts' Lolo guide, and together they equipped an expedition from the inventory her husband had assembled before he died. Along with the traps and ropes needed to capture a full-size animal, she carried with her a baby bottle and dry milk in case they should find a baby panda.

Ruth Harkness's account of hunting in the mountains echoes those of men far better prepared for the journey than she:

> In places the bamboo had fallen and
> made slimy wet traps into which I sank
> to my waist. The branches caught at my
> boot laces and it took every ounce of
> muscle I possessed to pull myself out.
> By that time I was proceeding mostly

on hands and knees, and only Yang [one of her guides] remained behind to give me an occasional lift by the seat of my pants.

Despite the difficulties, Ruth succeeded not only in securing a live baby panda, but in getting it safely back to the United States. She fed it a makeshift formula made from the dry milk and kept it warm in a bed made from the party's last clean shirts. The camp cook wove a bamboo pack basket to carry Su Lin—"a little something very cute"—down out of the mountains.

At Che'ng-tu, Ruth and Su Lin were lucky to be offered a ride to Shanghai aboard a private plane. "I'm going to be the first American pilot ever to fly a baby panda down to Shanghai as 'pidgin' cargo in the control room," the captain laughed. He was, in fact the first to fly a panda anywhere. After several weeks of red tape and a night up with a colicky panda, Ruth sailed for San Francisco.

The public uproar over the arrival of the first live panda was enormous. Ruth and Su Lin were

the first female guests of the Explorers Club (only much later was Su Lin discovered to be male). Newspaper clamored for interviews. Suddenly pandas were in style and eclipsed the teddy bear as America's favorite stuffed toy. Su Lin went to the Brookfield Zoo in Chicago, and Ruth returned to China in 1938 for another panda.

Ruth Harkness's success in securing Su Lin began another flurry of expeditions to capture live pandas for zoos instead of dead ones for museums. Pandora arrived at the Bronx Zoo just in time to become a celebrity in her own right as the 1939 World's Fair was opening in New York. St. Louis purchased a pair for their zoo shortly afterwards.

Tangier Smith, a professional hunter who had accused Ruth Harkness of buying Su Lin, caught a total of six pandas for zoos. By the late 1930s, a total of eleven pandas had been taken out of China alive and seven more had been shot. Worried about the depletion of an already rare animal, China restricted the exportation of pandas in 1939.

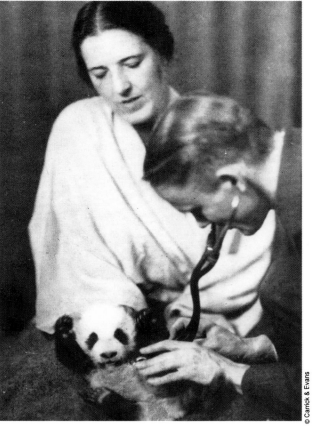

When Su Lin became colicky in Shanghai, Ruth called in a pediatrician—who said, "A pandor? Sounds disagreeable." But he came to her hotel and examined the infant giant panda.

## POLITICS AND PANDAS

Although hunting for foreign zoos was no longer allowed, the panda was to become China's ambassador of friendship. After Japan invaded China early in World War II, Americans responded generously to China's need for food and medical supplies through United China Relief.

As a thank-you gift to the children of America, Madame Chiang Kai-shek presented the Bronx Zoo with a pair of pandas, who were named Pandee and Pandah. The war in the Pacific was under way, and the pandas were flown in a blacked-out plane over Japanese-held territory to Kowloon, then out of Kowloon the day before the city was almost totally destroyed by bombing. During the pandas' voyage from the Philippines, the Japanese attacked Pearl Harbor, and the last half of the trip was made through seas filled with enemy ships. But the gift arrived safely, to the delight of American crowds who flocked to the Bronx Zoo to see the pandas.

In the 1960s, when East-West relations were

**The Washington Post**

WEDNESDAY, MAY 18, 1988

### Are China's Touring Pandas Being Loved to Death?

#### U.S. Groups Sue, Charging Commercial Exploitation

By Cass Peterson
Washington Post Staff Writer

Say what you will about the majestic lion, in the zoo world the giant panda is king. Nothing draws a crowd like the furry creatures with the endearing black eye patches and teddy-bear looks.

That is why former president Jimmy Carter put a word in for Zoo Atlanta during a recent visit to China and why New York Mayor Edward I. Koch lobbied heavily for panda visitors at the Bronx Zoo.

That also is why the Toledo Zoo imported LeLe and Nan Nan for the city's 150th anniversary celebration this year, a move that has placed the city in a heated dispute between wildlife groups and the Interior Department over whether the giant panda is literally being loved to death.

Concerned that the endangered panda is becoming the victim of commercial exploitation, the World Wildlife Fund and American Association of Zoological Parks and Aquariums (AAZPA) have sued to prevent Toledo from exhibiting the pandas, who arrived on a flight from Shanghai last week. The Toledo Zoological Society has countersued, charging restraint of trade.

At issue is the increasingly popular practice of short-term panda loans, ... dozens have been shipped ... temporary exhibit. Only a ... of China, including the ... have permanent panda ... ers say the touring ... vation by building ... species.

But opponen ... degenerated into ... trade, with potential ... the species.

In recent years, panda lo ... a significant source of hard ... China, which receives between ... and $500,000 for a typical 100-day ... Host zoos, meanwhile, stand to reap a ... stantial profit from increased admissions and sale of such panda-related trinkets as T-shirts, stuffed toys and ceramic mugs.

Most exhibitions have been held at public zoos, but the panda craze seems to be spreading. The Bronx pandas made a side trip to Busch Gardens in Florida, a popular

and Nan Nan, are of breeding age. Because China does not allow host zoos to attempt breed pandas, conservationists believe ... animals potentially capable of repro ... should not be on the tourist circuit.

AAZPA and the World Wildli ... which adopted the panda as its s ... than 26 years ago, charge in s ... the Interior Department w ... granting Toledo a permit ... imals.

Because as few as ... the wild, according ... Wildlife Service, ... tional treaty fo ... cial purposes ... Zoo has u ... featuring ... much an ... lot an

---

**The New York** ...

NEW YORK, APRIL 7, 1988

### China Is Said to Arrest 203 for Panda P...

April 6 (AP) — ... ople for ille- ... red giant ... repre- ...

Mr. Reilly said the announcement of the arrests, which was made in February by China's Forestry Minister, Gao Dezhan, was the first time China had publicized such detailed statistics.

China's last public estimate of the giant panda population — about 1,000 ... nals — was made in this year; results is announced only for the Wo- ... Preserve, where there ... 1976 and 72 now. ... il the February ... said poach- ... gh the ... for

The Chinese F ... portedly said 15 ... sought in connec ... tion into poaching ... chuan Province ... where almost all ... Twenty-six pe ... year to life, the ... quoted as having ... Some pandas ... snares set for a ... cies, the Asian ... valued in tradit ... Panda furs ... smuggled to Ho ... The wildlife ...

day ... min ... "T ... has ... said, ... the cu ... rat" a ... weight ... ity. If it ... could gr ... 300 poune ... Zoo of ... the mothe ... spring.

---

**Los Angeles Herald Examiner**

LOS ANGELES

August 22, 1987

### Pandas create zoo pandemonium

#### Irresistible animals boost attendance, preservation efforts

By Nancy Spiller
Herald staff writer

When the pandas came to town for a three-month visit, the Los Angeles Zoo's attendance increased 450,000 over its average annual of 1.5 million visitors. People stood in line for hours to see the pair for just a few minutes.

Pandas have become the blockbuster exhibit for zoos in the '80s.

The first pair of pandas to tour outside the People's Republic of China came here during the 1984 Olympics. This summer, there are four pairs on loan to zoos outside China. In Europe and two in the United States, two in April, a pair went on exhibit at New York's Bronx Zoo and in July, Basi and Yuan Yuan arrived from the Fuzhou Zoo for a 200-day stay in San Diego.

A symbiotic relationship between zoos and pandas results. "We have a loan agreement with the Chinese that is very beneficial to the San Diego Zoo," says George Risser, general director of the San Diego Zoo.

The zoological society "has elected not to reveal exactly how beneficial, but there will be a donation made to panda preservation efforts in China. Risser says the preservation and the adored pair to double attendance figures during their six-month stay. To handle the overflow, the San Diego Zoo has doubled its parking capacity, adding an additional 3,000 spaces.

"Everyone loves pandas," says Dr. Bruce W. Bunting, director of the World Wildlife Fund's Asia Program for ... in 1961, pandas have been the fund's mascot and symbol. The panda is one of the fund's most successful sellers in the line of ... animals ...

"It's one of the most popular species worldwide, and people have long identified with them," and ... Now that they're identified with endangered species, people begin to understand that preservation is not a simple issue. It also helps to hit home that there are ...

The frequent-flyer pandas may help pay the way for their less glamorous, ... brethren, but zoos work out deals so they benefit as well.

only 700 left worldwide. It's a great ambassador. I just wish North America had something as cute."

The sea otter probably comes closest to the cuteness of pandas but, "they're no longer endangered." The Florida panther, a subspecies of cougar, is endangered, but it's not something the public would necessarily want to cuddle up to.

San Diego has spent $500,000 on an air-conditioned "panda pad" that will remain when the pandas leave. The 200 hopes to cover these costs from revenues from panda souvenirs, all of which and the sale of into the 200's general operating fund.

The L.A. Zoo had a $250,000 China Pavilion built for the animals' stay, and the city of Los Angeles repaved roads at the zoo.

According to Lora LaMarca, spokeswoman for the Greater Los Angeles Zoo Association, "the pandas brought a lot of people to the zoo that wouldn't have come" and hadn't been there in a long time.

The L.A. Zoo donated $175,000 and hospital equipment to a panda preserve in China. A good portion of that came from the Panda Peril Fund donation box located near the exhibit.

Caught up in the throes of adoration, the public is probably never more ready to contribute to efforts to save pandas than when face to face with the irresistible mammals.

When the golden monkeys visited San Diego from China in 1985, a donation box was put by the display and $150,000 was collected for conservation. The public won't have the same opportunity with the pandas.

"There'll be no donation box nearby. We felt that our members had waited long enough for the pandas to arrive," Risser says. "We didn't want to ask them for anything additional."

The San Diego Zoo, like the Chinese ... success with koalas is allowing other zoos to have visiting ... maintain Australian exhibits of its own. Its package is a koala keeper and regular fresh shipments of eucalyptus, the koalas' sole diet. In a world in which the koalas are difficult to obtain for display, traveling ... have become increasingly rare and difficult freshen, the zoos mix ... endangered species exhibits

One of the two giant pandas on loan for 200 days ... the San Diego Zoo nibbles on a tidbit of bamboo.

less than cordial, the London and Moscow zoos (the only zoos outside China that had pandas) tried to arrange a private detente by sending the female Chi-Chi, from London to Moscow for mating. The zoos enjoyed more cordial relations than the principal figures in this blind date; Chi-Chi turned down Moscow's An-An flat and returned to London.

In 1972, United States President Richard M. Nixon traveled to China in a historic move to thaw previously strained relations between the two countries. The United States commemorated the visit, which led to the opening of diplomatic rela-

tions between the United States and The People's Republic of China, with the gift of two musk oxen to the Peking Zoo. China in turn presented the National Zoo in Washington, D.C., with a pair of pandas, Ling-Ling and Hsing-Hsing, that have become the most famous Chinese ambassadors of all time.

These two pandas have also sparked several continuing cooperative programs between the two countries on behalf of panda conservation. Everywhere pandas travel, they not only make friends, but they make people more interested in their future safety.

# WORLD TRAVELERS AND AMBASSADORS: PANDAS IN ZOOS

As China's ambassadors of goodwill, pandas have been presented to zoos in London, Moscow, Tokyo, Paris, Mexico City, Madrid, and West Berlin, as well as to the National Zoo in Washington, D.C. A number of others have visited zoos as houseguests on loan for special exhibits. Chi-Chi, who eventually took up residence at Regent's Park Zoo in London, had first toured Frankfurt, Copenhagen, and Berlin.

Since Su Lin's journey via pack basket, small plane, ocean liner, and train, pandas have traveled in a variety of ways. Tangier Smith, the most successful of the zoo hunters, fre-

Though the first pandas taken from China did not survive long, we now know more about caring for them. Those that have arrived in recent years have adapted relatively easily to new surroundings.

quently "exported" his catch inside caravans of empty oil trucks. But the official gifts have traveled in considerably more style ever since Mme. Chiang's gift dodged submarines while crossing the Pacific.

Hsing-Hsing and Ling-Ling arrived in Washington, D.C., on Sunday, April 16, 1972 from Beijing in two pale-green lacquered crates aboard a special cargo plane. Each crate was inscribed in both Chinese and English "Giant Panda presented from the Beijing Municipal Revolutionary Committee, The People's Republic of China." The pandas were escorted by three Chinese government officials and Yang Cheng-fu, chief panda keeper at the Beijing Zoo. The pandas seemed no worse for their travels, except that they spent a few days setting their internal "clocks" to Eastern Standard Time—the same problem East-West travelers have encountered since the dawn of the jet age.

The pandas on loan to the Bronx Zoo in 1987 arrived in even grander style, aboard a 747—in the cabin, of course. Thirteen hours was too long for such distinguished passengers to spend in a baggage hold.

For animals that have so little variety in their natural environments, pandas adjust remarkably well to life in zoos. Almost the instant the barred door of her travel crate was opened, Ling-Ling was out and exploring her new home at the National Zoo in Washington, D.C. She inspected everything, found her water pan, and immediately turned it upside down over her head.

From their first meal of rice porridge, cornmeal, milk, apples, and carrots, the newly arrived pandas ate well and were soon settled into the zoo's routine. During the four days between their arrival and the official presentation ceremony, Ling-Ling completely dissected the potted bamboo plants in her enclosure and spent the rest of her time performing hand-stands in the pots.

Hsing-Hsing enjoys a nice thick stem of bamboo at the National Zoo.

© Jessie Cohen/National Zoological Park

© Chase Roe

When Mrs. Nixon and the press arrived for the ceremonies, they were greeted by a very active black-and-brown Ling-Ling and a more traditionally colored but sleeping Hsing-Hsing, who was still recovering from jet lag. Ling-Ling, for all her murky appearance, performed as many tricks as she could think of for the group of American and Chinese dignitaries—as good an ambassador as any nation could have chosen to break the ice in the cold war.

Although most pandas have settled in quickly, adapting to new surroundings, companions, and schedules easily, occasionally one does not. In 1988, when Chia-Chia was in transit from London to the Chapultepec Zoo in Mexico City, he stopped off for a three-month stay in the Cincinnati Zoo. After his seventeen-hour trip from London, he paced uneasily,

With their meals provided by a friendly zookeeper, giant pandas in captivity have time on their hands to climb and play. (Below) Ling-Ling takes in the view from a favorite perch.

© Jessie Cohen/National Zoological Park

panting and obviously agitated. Zoo officials quickly realized that the problem was more than jet lag when Chia-Chia became irate when a keeper closed the door to his den. Inside, the officials remembered, was Chia-Chia's only link with his London home of fourteen years: his familiar bedding. Jo Gipps, London's panda expert, summed up Chia-Chia's problem succinctly: "Homesick is exactly the word!"

Despite the consistently cool weather conditions of their native habitat, pandas in captivity seem to adapt quickly to different climates—except for the hot, muggy one of Washington, D.C. in July. But a few blocks of ice in Hsing-Hsing's and Ling-Ling's enclosures soon brought them back to their playful selves, as they slid on them and chipped off pieces to toss in the air, rub on their fur, or eat. By the time Andrews Air Force Base personnel arrived with a giant portable air conditioner, the pandas were already cool and happy.

Lien Ho, on his way to London as a gift after the war, had a similar experience in Calcutta when his plane made a stopover. The temperature was hovering around 100° F. (38° C.) and he was miserable, having just left the snowy mountains. An ice factory took Lien Ho in, and he spent the stopover comfortably, leaving with several blocks of ice for the remainder of the trip.

The panda environment at the Toledo Zoo included a flowing stream and rocks with air conditioners inside them that blew cool air out through a grate to help the animals stay comfortable in what was for them unusually hot weather.

© Sharon Cummings

© World Wildlife Fund/Don Reid

# THE CARE AND FEEDING OF PANDAS IN ZOOS

Life in the zoo is much easier for pandas than life in the wild, since at home most waking hours are spent looking for food and eating. The zoo diet is easier to digest and richer in nutrients than bamboo, so captive pandas have time and energy left over for playing, which they do very creatively.

Zoos take different attitudes toward the panda's diet. At the National Zoo, in Washington, D.C., pandas eat sweet potatoes, kale, Milkbones, cat food, vitamin and mineral supplements, and, of course, bamboo along with rice, cornmeal, apples, and carrots. There are occasional treats of bread and honey, especially when keepers need to lure the pandas into or out of their dens. But the pandas' diets are carefully measured and monitored for nutrient balance.

Bamboo is grown in Rock Creek Park, where the National Zoo is located, but it is carefully monitored for lead levels because of the city traf-

fic. The West Berlin Zoo, like the National Zoo, prepares panda meals in a separate kitchen, and has bamboo flown in regularly from France on a special plane.

At the other end of the range in professional opinion on panda feeding is the Chapultepec Zoo in Mexico City. "We don't worry too much about special panda diets," an official there says. "We just feed them what they like." When asked what that was, the official grinned. "Barbecued chicken!" Considering that Mexico City has had more success with breeding pandas than any other zoo outside China, maybe there is a lesson to be learned.

Keeping such a rare animal healthy is a constant concern for zoos. Before the pair of pandas arrived at the National Zoo in Washington, an entire building had been renovated for them. There were two separate areas with thick glass walls, remote controlled sliding doors, and air conditioning. Everything was scrubbed and scrubbed again to be sure it was free of any bacterial remains of its former occupants—four bongos and a pair of white rhinos.

Panda habits are recorded carefully and records are kept of their weight and size, with

This panda at the Calgary Zoo is being fed a gruel of rice and milk that contains its daily supplemental vitamins. Pandas are very fond of this mixture and are liable to become obese from the unusually high calorie intake.

occasional laboratory analysis of urine samples. Although the Chinese have done considerable work in training pandas to climb onto scales and cooperate in other medical procedures, Washington's zookeepers simply take advantage of their natural curiosity and roll a scale into their enclosure. The pandas will immediately climb onto the scale to investigate. In West Berlin, the panda's bed is a scale, so weight can be recorded nightly.

Loss of appetite or weight is an important clue to the panda's health. Like most wild animals, the panda rarely looks or acts sick, since this would alert predators to a weakened state and invite attack.

The diagnosis of disease in pandas or in other large and potentially dangerous animals is tricky at best. Some fairly routine tests can be carried out easily, but those who work with pandas are constantly conscious of their strength and sharp claws. Keepers have been seriously injured by

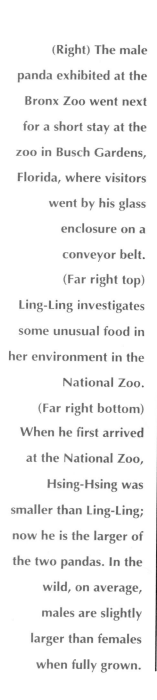

(Right) The male panda exhibited at the Bronx Zoo went next for a short stay at the zoo in Busch Gardens, Florida, where visitors went by his glass enclosure on a conveyor belt. (Far right top) Ling-Ling investigates some unusual food in her environment in the National Zoo. (Far right bottom) When he first arrived at the National Zoo, Hsing-Hsing was smaller than Ling-Ling; now he is the larger of the two pandas. In the wild, on average, males are slightly larger than females when fully grown.

© Sharon Cummings

© Jessie Cohen/National Zoological Park

pandas in the past, and a panda's idea of play can be quite rough.

Complicated procedures and those that involve drawing blood require that the animals be anesthetized. Unfortunately, this adds stress to an already sick animal.

In December 1983, Ling-Ling contracted an infection of the lower urinary tract that did not respond to antibiotics. Using a blowdart, an instrument used with elephants and other big game on African reserves, zoo doctors anesthetized Ling-Ling. All tests were normal except her blood count. She was seriously anemic, with a red cell count of 10 percent instead of the normal 40 percent. Without immediate help, she might not even wake up from the anesthesia.

There was no time to get blood from any panda except Hsing-Hsing, so he too was anesthetized and had his blood tested. He was healthy and able to donate. With careful monitoring to spot any reaction to incompatible blood, Ling-Ling was given a transfusion. At this point things were pretty tense in the Panda House, since Ling-Ling's immune system might begin to destroy Hsing-Hsing's precious red blood cells. She was given cortisone injections, and her white count remained steady.

A sample of bone marrow tested showed discouraging results. The marrow showed that Ling-Ling's body was not responding to the transfusion and producing new red blood cells in the normal fashion. In further tests that measured her kidney

© Jessie Cohen/National Zoological Park

Nan-Nan and Le-Le, the subadult panda pair exhibited at the Toledo Zoo, were taken from the wild when they were quite young, during the bamboo die-off in 1983, and have cohabitated off and on ever since.

functions, her serum creatinine level, which should be under 1.5, was 19.5; Ling-Ling's kidneys were not cleansing her blood properly.

Nephrologists from the Children's Hospital National Medical Center were called in, and veterinarians at the London Zoo were contacted for advice. A kidney biopsy and other tests were performed while the creatinine test was repeated. The level was down to 3.7 and her red cell count was beginning to rise.

The source of the problem was discovered to be a bacterial infection of the kidney tubules; her kidneys were not irreversibly damaged and were otherwise still healthy and able to function. Everyone at the National Zoo breathed a sigh of relief that was echoed in zoos everywhere.

It was a hard way to learn, but at least zoo officials found out that they could mobilize a team of experts on very short notice when a life-threatening illness struck. Ling-Ling's illness also added considerably to the knowledge of panda medicine. Each zoo's experience in keeping their charges healthy adds little by little to what is known about the panda. With so few pandas left, each scrap of information could someday be crucial to their survival.

London's Panda Pavilion includes a complete research station, and discoveries there, as well as observations at all other facilities, are shared by panda-owning zoos throughout the world. When it looked like Ling-Ling might require another transfusion, Chia-Chia stood ready in London.

© Sharon Cummings

# BREEDING IN ZOOS

Of all the panda's puzzling qualities, the one that continues to confound experts is their problem with breeding in captivity. Or, more precisely, why are zoos so unsuccessful at breeding pandas?

Early attempts to breed pandas in captivity failed due to some very basic errors. The pair Mme. Chiang presented to the Bronx Zoo never mated, and on the animals' deaths, in 1945 and 1951 respectively, both were found to be females. Mistakes in sexing had occurred with Su Lin and with Lien Ho in London as well. Clearly zoos would have to learn more about pandas before they could entertain notions of breeding!

But determining pandas' sex hasn't been the sole difficulty. The St. Louis Zoo had a mixed pair that for seven years failed to produce the patter of little panda paws. Meanwhile, European zoos, despite breeding loans, were just as unsuccessful.

The flat rejection London's Chi-Chi dealt Moscow's An-An was thought to be the result of Chi-Chi's long isolation from other pandas and constant companionship with her human keepers. Wary, keepers at the National Zoo were careful not to let pandas become too dependent upon humans for company.

Having two pandas in one zoo on a permanent basis should also have eliminated the traumas of travel, unfamiliar surroundings, and sudden encounters with strange pandas. Hsing-Hsing and Ling-Ling, at the National Zoo, were in neighboring enclosures separated only by a link fence. They were allowed to explore each other's enclosures, although only when the other was in its pen.

By 1972, the Chinese scientists who had accompanied Ling-Ling and Hsing-Hsing to the United States explained another problem they had discovered in their work: Both pandas must be in season simultaneously in order for mating to occur. (In the wild this seems to be less of a problem than it is in captivity.)

By 1980, both pandas had certainly reached maturity, and they had been at the zoo long enough for keepers to have observed them over several mating seasons. But they had failed to mate. A number of reasons were suggested—everything from diet to shyness. William A. Xangten, Jr. describes the attempts in the May–June, 1980 *Zoogoer:*

Hsing-Hsing and Ling-Ling are kept in separate enclosures, except during breeding season, and can often be seen trying to communicate through the fence.

© Peter B. Kaplan/Photo Researchers, Inc.

© Sharon Cummings

Nan-Nan and Le-Le, visitors at the Toledo Zoo, seemed to enjoy playing and wrestling together whenever they could.

For what we thought might be the *real* problems, we did what we could. We thought they needed more time— we gave them time. The Chinese suggested that they might be too heavy— we put them both on diets, and they both lost weight. Ling-Ling went from a plump 296 pounds (134 kilograms) to a svelte 242 (110). Their diet wasn't proper? Well, we didn't give them oysters and champagne, but we did provide the optimum vitamins, minerals, and proteins, plus lots of vitamin E. Were they being given too much time? We shortened the encounter periods.

Nothing seemed to work. Why wouldn't they breed?

Who could have known that the problem wasn't physical, but psychological?

In their encounters, Hsing-Hsing had begun to dominate more and more. At first, when Ling-Ling rebuffed him, he stopped trying, but by the 1977, '78 and '79 mating seasons, he had become more persistent, backing off for a few minutes, then approaching again. But when Ling-Ling tired of his attentions, she simply rolled over on her side, making mating impossible.

Dr. John Eisenberg, the National Zoo's assistant director for animal programs, described Hsing-Hsing diplomatically as "maladroit." As early as 1979 the zoo realized that it might need to follow Chinese experience and attempt artificial insemination. This is a fallback position, since it entails anesthetizing both animals, always somewhat risky with large mammals. But nature's course certainly wasn't working.

In June 1979 the zoo called in Dr. Stephen Seager of Texas A & M University, an expert on the artificial insemination of exotic animals. Hsing-Hsing was electroejaculated twice in three days, and the semen was tested, frozen in liquid nitrogen, and stored at $-320°$ ($-160°$C). Samples were tested for viability during the year and found to be 80 percent alive a year later.

When Ling-Ling came into heat in May 1980, natural mating was tried first but again failed. Dr.

Theodore Reed, then zoo director, described the problem: "She was willing and he was anxious, but they just couldn't coordinate their efforts." Rarely have the intimate details of a couple's private lives been so closely watched or publicly discussed!

Hoping to use fresh semen, doctors anesthetized Hsing-Hsing, but his sperm count was too low after his unsuccessful attempt at mating earlier in the day. This discovery did, however, add an important bit of information to the record: Male pandas require twenty-four hours to fully recover their sperm count. This makes the chances of natural mating even slimmer, since the female egg is thought to be viable for only twelve hours. With estrus, or heat, occurring only once a year and having to be concurrent between both animals, the chances of successful natural mating seem very slim indeed.

When Hsing-Hsing had completely recovered (only in a near-desperate lifesaving attempt will the zoo anesthetize both animals at the same time), Ling-Ling was inseminated with the stored semen. But despite zoo preparations and hopes throughout the world for a baby panda, nothing happened.

Zookeepers from China accompanied Nan-Nan and Le-Le to the United States and watched the animals' interactions closely at all times.

The next spring, Chia-Chia, the male from the London Zoo came to Washington, but he and Ling-Ling were not compatible and he went home again. In 1982, Hsing-Hsing and Ling-Ling spent time together but failed to mate. Ling-Ling was again artificially inseminated and everyone took hope as she began to show behavioral indications of pregnancy—including loss of appetite, changed hormones in her urine and nest building. But there was no baby.

Since the panda's gestation period is of indefinite length and the panda shows no outward physical signs of pregnancy until just before the birth, all a zoo can do is watch and wait and be sure that everything is ready just in case.

In 1983, the zoo decided to hedge its bets. The pandas at long last mated naturally on March 18, but the zoo decided also to artificially inseminate Ling-Ling with semen from Chia-Chia in London. By July, Ling-Ling's urine samples showed high levels of hormones that corresponded with those recorded in Madrid, where a female panda had given birth in 1982.

Once pregnancy was suspected, the Panda House was closed to visitors and volunteers from Friends of the National Zoo (FONZ) began a

After years of failed attempts at mating and artificial insemination, Ling-Ling finally became pregnant.

© Peter B. Kaplan/Photo Researchers, Inc.

© Sharon Cummings

Don Reid explains an alternative approach to breeding pandas in captivity: "Generally, we have kept pandas separately in captivity because that is how they seem to live in the wild—and I think that's a mistake. Since subadult pandas do sometimes live together in the wild, maybe if we put subadults together in captivity, and let them grow up together, breeding would be more successful. I think the animals can be compatible in captivity as long as they have a big enough space so they can find privacy when they need it—which isn't often the case. We've put them in too small a space and then they get ornery and start fighting, and the vets worry that they're going to hurt each other, so they pull them apart. But that doesn't need to be the process. We've had a lot of problems mating other wild or endangered animals and solutions have developed after experimentation—especially with female mate choices, that is, putting females with different males throughout the year, letting them get used to each other, and then allowing the females to make a choice between those males come breeding time. That way *they* have the choice. They can certainly discern subtle differences a lot better than we can."

Though her first panda cub survived only three hours, the birth demonstrated that Ling-Ling can conceive and has strong maternal instincts. In these scenes from the birth videotape, the baby cries, and she responds to its call, gently licking it and taking it into her mouth.

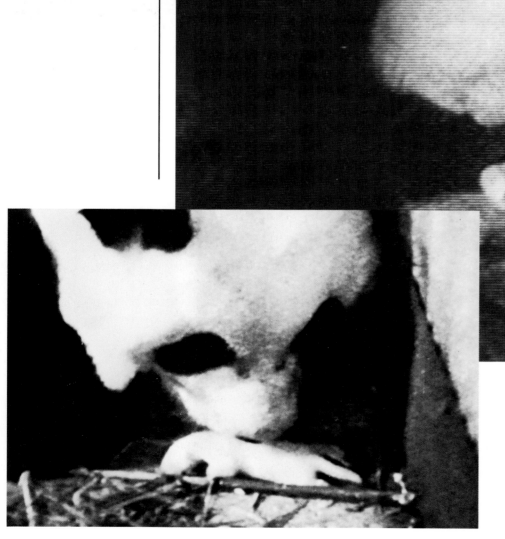

twenty-four-hour around-the-clock watch, recording Ling-Ling's every action with video equipment donated by the National Geographic Society. Visitors couldn't see Ling-Ling at this time, but they could watch through a TV monitor in the education building.

Ling-Ling built a nest of bamboo and tensions grew. At 3:18 A.M. on July 21, Ling-Ling gave

birth. FONZ volunteer Roberta Baskin, on duty at the time with Collection Manager Bess Frank and Keeper Barbara Bingham, described the experience: "I was really a wreck! I had done only one other shift on the watch. I was really glad that Bess and Barbara were there, because they had more experience with the camera. I was afraid I'd miss taping the birth or have the whole thing out of focus!"

Baskin was still on duty at 6:25 A.M., while the zoo staff was busy answering calls from reporters and preparing for the 11 A.M. press conference. The baby had been vigorous and noisy, and Ling-Ling was holding it. Baskin described in *Zoogoer* what happened next: "She just let it go. She had been licking it quite a bit and then she let go. I was just crushed." Watchers knew that the long-awaited cub was dead only three hours after its birth. The cause of death was established as pneumonia developed before the cub was born, perhaps stemming from a bacterial infection sometime earlier in the birth canal.

Even from this tragedy, a lot of new information emerged. There were the detailed records of the pregnancy and birth, as well as the autopsy information. To scientists, the most significant discov-ery was the result of the zoo's curiosity over the parentage of the cub. Since Ling-Ling had received semen naturally from Hsing-Hsing and artificially from Chia-Chia, they wanted to know which panda was the father. It was in the course of this investigation that Dr. Stephen O'Brien at the National Cancer Institute concluded that the panda was more closely related to the bear than to the raccoon (see page 27). They also gave Hsing-Hsing's image a boost by establishing that he was the father.

The two pandas' mating problems seemed to have been solved, and the summer following the breakthrough Ling-Ling gave birth to a stillborn cub. Another was stillborn in 1987. In 1988 hopes once again ran high, but she experienced a false pregnancy.

With each year's mating season comes knowledge, and the National Zoo has greatly improved its chances of avoiding opportunistic infections, a problem at all zoos. The Panda House has been remodeled to make it less likely to harbor bacteria, and porous surfaces have been coated with sealer. Water supplies and cleaning procedures have been improved.

Zoo Pathologist Dr. Richard Montali discov-

"If you get close to a panda about eight months old like this one," says Don Reid, "the first thing it will do is pull your fingers into its mouth." Young pandas also seem to have an instinctive desire to use their forelimbs for climbing.

ered that panda cubs have little ability to fight off infection; they are a living breeding ground, just waiting for some bacteria to find them and multiply. As a result of this discovery, during what turned out to be a false pregnancy in 1988 the doctors were ready with gamma globulin, prepared from Hsing-Hsing's blood, to be administered immediately as a boost to activate the newborn's immune system.

Research and monitoring techniques improve continually, too. The National Zoo, for instance, has an entirely new TV system donated by the National Geographic Society and Sony Corporation of America. Its eight cameras are complete with pan, zoom, and tilt controls; six microphones; ten monitors; and three recorders, all connected by miles of wiring. The system can work even in complete darkness.

"It's live and learn when it comes to pandas," says the National Zoo's collection manager, Lisa Stevens. "The only hard part is having to wait almost a whole year for the next season to begin!"

Along with the Madrid panda (the mother there has since died), cubs born in Mexico City's Chapultepec Zoo have survived infancy and the first has grown to breeding age. Meanwhile, in 1963, China's first panda conceived in captivity was born, and in 1978 the Chinese had their first successful birth from artificial insemination.

Fifteen of the twenty-two pandas born at the Beijing Zoo have survived; the last eight of these were the product of artificial insemination.

# WHAT ZOOS HAVE LEARNED ABOUT PANDAS

In addition to the information on breeding, disease, medical treatment, and cubs, scientists have learned a lot about the intelligence, personality, and social behavior of pandas by watching them in zoos.

Pandas are among the most playful of wild animals. As mothers, they are tireless in their patience with cubs, teaching them and preparing them for life in the wild. Adult pandas without cubs to train seem to play just for enjoyment, and keepers insist that many of their antics are performed with an eye to the audience. At the National Zoo, whenever the pandas are outdoors at the same time and can see each other, their antics seem to increase. They do headstands and somersaults and roll down the hill in their enclosures.

When hot weather in Washington made keepers nervous about letting Ling-Ling and Hsing-Hsing spend too much time out-of-doors, the National Zoo decided to try giving them swim-

Hsing-Hsing (top) and Ling-Ling (bottom) during one of their familiarization visits.

© Sharon Cummings

**Giant pandas are strong animals that move slowly most of the time.**

ming pools. Natural instinct, still fairly strong even in captive-born pandas, prompted Ling-Ling to approach her pool carefully from down wind. She was soon basking in the pool, with her head and feet sticking out the top of the tub.

Several zoos provide swings made of truck tires suspended from chains, and pandas spend many hours playing on these—crawling through, swinging, and doing flips from tire to ground.

Pandas love to play with balls, but finding one they aren't able to tear to shreds has proved to be a real problem. Basketballs, even extra-tough ones, last two days at the most. Eventually FONZ volunteers went to an industrial research firm and had them design a high-tech ball of extruded laminated plastic with riveted sections. It lasted a few months before Ling-Ling got her teeth through it. An even more complicated replacement lasted only two hours. Specially designed larger balls,

too big to get a grip on, last about six months.

But even without toys, pandas are quick to find diversion. The disc of ice from a frozen water dish; the pots that bamboo is planted in; and trees, shrubs, fences, or anything within reach become toys.

In Chinese zoos and in the Shanghai Circus, pandas are trained to do tricks and acrobatics. They are adept at balancing on balls and riding rocking horses and even bicycles with training wheels. They have been taught to push baby carriages, eat with silverware, and play trumpets. While the Chinese use pandas as circus performers, the animals' training is not just frivolous. Using techniques learned in training pandas to perform, the Fuzhou Zoo has taught the animals to lie down on command and to receive medical treatment. The trained pandas will sit quietly while they are weighed, examined, and given

EKGs. (The latter is usually done only on pandas under restraint or sedation which not only gives inaccurate results, but increases the trauma and places the patient at greater risk.) In January 1982, Quing-Quing of Fuzhou was given a transfusion with no sedation and lay quietly for about an hour without disturbing the needle or the bottle.

From the relatively few pandas available for study it is hard to determine the panda's intelligence with any certainty. Also, ascribing intelligence in animals is risky at best, since we really don't now why they do what they do. What might appear to be intelligence could merely be instinct or curiosity, while apparent lack of intelligence might be lack of experience.

There is no doubt that pandas recognize different humans and form bonds of affection or dependence with them. Su Lin, after two months at the Brookfield Zoo without seeing Ruth Harkness, recognized her captor's voice and jumped a fence to reach her, landing in her arms.

Keepers are quick, however, to relate experiences of trying to match wits with pandas. When Ling-Ling wanted the sliding door between her den and enclosure left open (it worked by remote control), she simply put her head in its path or held it open with a powerful paw.

When they are unable to reach something, pandas often push a mobile object to a position where they can climb on it. Pandas are also very quick to discover any weakness or oversight in the security of their enclosures: a crevice in a wall that provides a foothold, or a tree limb from which they can reach the fence. Even very young pandas are quick to find ways to beat the system, and keepers agree that they have trouble staying one step ahead of them.

Like other slow moving animals, giant pandas were once considered unintelligent. However, the more we learn the less that assumption appears to be true.

# chapter

# WHERE THE PANDAS ARE

## four

hile zoo panda populations do change, the group of zoos that have pandas tends to remain fairly constant. London, for example, has had a succession of pandas, and Mexico City seems assured of a continuing supply for some years. While more zoos may obtain them in the future and many captive pandas currently travel on loan, the zoos outside the orient where travelers are most likely to see the animals are in Washington, Madrid, Paris, West Berlin, and Mexico City.

Before making a trip with the special purpose of seeing pandas at these zoos, it is wise to check with the zoo or with the National Tourist Office of the country involved. Chia-Chia, the London zoo's only panda, may still be in Mexico City on an indefinite breeding loan, or if a female panda is about to give birth, she will not be on display to the public. So going to the right zoo is not a guarantee of seeing a panda.

The best time to visit, when pandas are likely to be most active, is at feeding time—frequently early in the morning when the zoo has just opened. Since crowds tend to be smaller in early morning, it is a good time for photography, too. Some zoos have specific panda viewing hours as well.

**Pandas attract more people to zoos than any other animal.**

# PHOTOGRAPHING PANDAS

Although each zoo has its own barrier system, each of which presents its particular challenges to photographers, there are ways to maximize photo successes. First, use a telephoto or zoom lens, since the pandas will rarely be close enough for a good portrait without one of these.

If there is no option but to photograph through a glass or plexiglass barrier, put the lens right up against the barrier if possible. An inexpensive flexible rubber lens shade will seal the area around the lens, cutting out all reflections. If an additional barrier prevents getting right up to the glass, a polarizing lens will cut out the reflections that otherwise could ruin a picture. If the photograph is taken indoors, a flash may or may not be allowed. Fast film (400 ASA) will usually eliminate the need for a flash. If using a flash, be sure to stand at an angle to the glass to avoid photographing the reflection of the flash.

Chain-link fences are another problem, but again, by going right up to them and putting the lens through one of the holes, it's possible to shoot right through. If a close approach is not possible, focus on the panda and shoot at a setting that minimizes depth-of-field. Set your camera's f-stop to the lowest number possible (widest aperture). This will make the fence so out-of-focus that it will appear, if at all, as a faint blur. Be patient and keep trying; taking a lot of pictures at different angles and settings will increase the chance of getting some really good ones.

Taking a photograph of a panda in China, where bamboo is as much an obstruction as a chain-link fence, is fortuitous at best.

Chia-Chia at Regents

Park Zoo in London.

# THE ZOOS

### London: Gardens of the Zoological Society of London

Located in North London inside Regents Park, this zoo is not easy to get to by public transportation. The nearest Tube station is Baker Street, from which most visitors walk through the park to reach the zoo. It is also possible to take a taxi from the subway to the entrance. The zoo is open daily until 6 P.M. in the summer or until dusk in the winter. Because of the hefty admission charge, be sure to check that Chia-Chia is back from Mexico City before going to the London Zoo.

### West Berlin: The Zoologischer Garten in the Tiergarten

Right in downtown Berlin, the zoo is reached through magnificent elephant gates on the Budapest-strasse, at the end of Kurfurstendamm, Berlin's main street. Beautifully kept animals are well-housed in interesting displays in a park setting. To get there by the underground, look for the Zoologischer Garten stop on the U-1 and U-9 lines.

## Paris: Jardin de Vincennes

The Jardin de Vincennes is one of the best places for photography, since there are no barriers in the way. The pandas are fed at about 9:30 A.M., a good time for viewing. To get there, take the #8 Metro line in the direction of Charenton-Ecoles and get off at the Porte Dorée station. Although the park is in Vincennes, *don't* take the #1 line to Château de Vincennes. The #8 line stops at Opéra, Montmartre, Républic, and several other major stations.

## Madrid: Zoo de la Casa de Campo

Madrid's is the only European zoo where a panda has been born. The Madrid zoo is also good for photography, with a diverse population of other species as well as the panda. The Metro stop is marked *Batan* and is located right in the Casa de Campo, a large public park on the outskirts of the city.

The pandas in the Jardin de Vincennes in Paris have a large natural environment separated from visitors by a moat.

### Washington, D.C.: The National Zoological Park
Located in Rock Creek Park in Northwest Washington not far from the center of the city, the National Zoo is a compact, easy-to-visit facility. The park is open from 8 A.M. to 8 P.M. with the buildings open from 9 A.M. to 6 P.M. Set along the steep slopes of a ravine, the park is well arranged, but the terrain can be difficult for anyone who has trouble climbing stairs. The pandas, however, are near the main entrance and require no strenuous walking to visit. They can be seen in two different viewing areas—outside in the mornings, when they are most active, and indoors during the afternoons. The pandas are fed at 11 A.M. and 3 P.M., and the public is welcome to watch.

**A visiting panda at the Bronx Zoo in New York City.**

© Michael George/Bruce Coleman Inc.

### Tokyo: Ueno Zoo
In the Ueno section of Tokyo, where many of the museums are located, the zoo is a short walk from the Ueno station on the Yamanote railway line. There is a pair of pandas whose quarters are near the main entrance. Although this is not one of the world's finest or most attractive zoos (many of the animals are in tiny, cramped cages), the pandas fare better than some with a large garden which visitors view through a glass wall. The best time to see the pandas is on weekdays, because on weekends over 20,000 people a day visit the zoo if the weather is good. It is open from 9:00 A.M. to 4:00 P.M. everyday except Monday when it is closed.

# THE RESERVES

Visiting the pandas in their native mountains of China requires both patience and determination. There are twelve panda reserves in China, but only the Wolong reserve is currently open to tourists and the only pandas to see are those in the breeding facility, since wild pandas are very hard to find and there is no reserve staff to guide visitors through the rough terrain.

From time to time, research or conservation organizations, such as the Sierra Club, arrange treks that include the reserve. Because these groups are prepared to camp, or are sponsors of the reserve in some way, they can sometimes stay in the area overnight. Several of the adventure travel outfitters, such as Overseas Adventure Travel in Cambridge, Massachusetts, may also include panda reserves in future itineraries, but because of the nature of the region and the purpose of the reserve, tourists in any number will never be allowed or encouraged.

Visitors can see beautiful scenes in the breeding facility in the Wolong Reserve, but tourism must be handled very carefully. Don Reid explains: "Tourist activity must benefit the local economy in order to have a positive impact on conservation. If tourism is perceived as a disturbance without benefit, local people are going to become disgruntled, and essentially, increased poaching will be the result."

# THE
# PANDA'S
# FUTURE

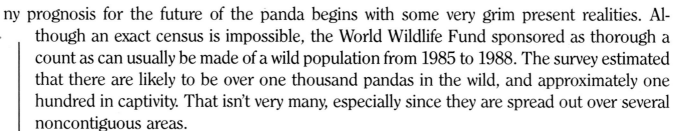

ny prognosis for the future of the panda begins with some very grim present realities. Although an exact census is impossible, the World Wildlife Fund sponsored as thorough a count as can usually be made of a wild population from 1985 to 1988. The survey estimated that there are likely to be over one thousand pandas in the wild, and approximately one hundred in captivity. That isn't very many, especially since they are spread out over several noncontiguous areas.

Only fifteen giant pandas reside in zoos outside China. Inside China, there may be more than eighty spread over thirty zoos and the Shanghai Circus, and a few more in breeding farms on reserves.

As important as panda numbers is the direction in which those numbers are changing. While the current figures show little difference from the number counted in the 1970s, the recent census was a far more rigorous and accurate study—a three-year cooperative project

Two pandas relax in the moat surrounding their environment in the Peking Zoo in China.

© George Holton/Photo Researchers, Inc.

between four divisions of the Chinese government, led by Shaokaiqing of the Szechwan forest bureau and Dr. Ken Johnson of the University of Tennessee. Chances are very good that the previous count missed far more pandas, which means that in the 1970s there were probably significantly more pandas than the 1,000 total counted.

Evidence from several sources shows a decline in wild populations. Records at Mount Emei from early in this century indicate that pandas lived in the forests above the temple there. As late as 1948, local newspapers mentioned them; now there are none. Local people who live near reserves and known habitats report seeing fewer and fewer pandas. Even more alarming, all the sightings have been of mature adults, not of cubs, which used to be reported. In the Fuping Reserve, staff identified only sixteen pandas during a six-month survey, of which only two were cubs.

Some scientists feel that the panda may have been doomed to extinction by the forces of

© Ken Johnson

evolution long before man intervened to either hasten or delay the inevitable. In other words, the panda may be a remnant species. The American Association of Zoological Parks and Aquarium (AAZPA) mentions this in its position statement:

> The emerging picture of the panda in nature, which will soon be clarified by a new study, is that of a dying species. Its wild populations appear too small and too fragmented to long survive without extraordinary efforts in species and habitat protection . . .

Other scientists, however, are not so pessimistic. They see the panda's problems as mostly human-generated and believe that those same humans can save the few remaining pandas and, with them, repopulate the wild. But believing that it *can* be done doesn't lead all of these scientists to believe that it *will* be done. Several stumbling blocks, some of them practical matters and others honest differences of opinion, plague the various groups whose responsibility it is to save the pandas.

The nature and consequence of the threats themselves is the best place to start when assessing the situation. In brief, these are: the destruction of habitat, limited diet, infrequent mating and breeding, island populations, poaching, disease, and the pressures of captivity. Each threat presents its own problems, but taken singly, none would probably be insurmountable. Together, they combine to create situations that are difficult to control.

The destruction of the panda's habitat is not a recent phenomenon. The Chinese have increased rapidly in population over the past several centuries and have pushed farther and farther into the previously wild areas to the west and south of the former major population centers. Since 1900 the population of the province of Szechwan alone has increased from 45 million to 150 million.

As the forest in the panda's habitat is destroyed, so too are the large, hollow fir trees they use for maternal dens. Because pandas give birth at the end of monsoon season (August to September) and cubs are so helpless at birth, protection improves the chances of a successful birth immensely.

As the people increased, they cut forests, squeezing the panda's habitat into small areas in the higher altitudes over 6,500 feet (1,981 meters). Agriculture has expanded closer and closer to these high areas, and the once-great forests that provided food and shelter for pandas even in the early years of this century have been cut. By the 1960s, national development became a top priority in China, and clear-cutting began in earnest. Roads and tunnels were built to provide access to all but the steepest and most remote places, and even more land was cleared for lumber and agriculture. Finally, the pandas were left only isolated pockets of the bamboo forests on widely separated high peaks. Even after the Chinese government set aside as 2,200 square miles (5,698 square kilometers) of the remaining 11,600 square miles (30,044 square kilometers) of panda range as reserves, the cutting continued.

The results have been both obvious and insidious. On the surface, we can see that the less panda land available, the more crowded and fragmented the panda populations will be in their search for bamboo. Pandas will eat other things besides bamboo, and some scientists

© World Wildlife Fund/Don Reid

(Far Left) Conservation plans include replanting forest trees and bamboo on existing farmland to create corridors connecting panda habitats. (Left) Evening light over the steep mountain valleys and subalpine forests where pandas make their home in the Wolong Reserve.

think that as the population and agricultural areas have expanded, cutting out other low altitude bamboos and other plants and bulbs, the panda's diet choices have been limited.

The dangers of this overspecialized diet became evident in 1975, and again in 1983, when the prevalent species of bamboo in panda territory flowered and died. Each species of bamboo has its own flowering cycle, ranging from fifteen to 120 years, depending on the species. After flowering, all the bamboo dies at once, leaving no food for the panda for several years until new growth is established. Historically, pandas have survived when a whole valley or mountainside of bamboo died at once; they simply moved to another place and ate a different variety. But with the bamboo forests now smaller, isolated, and widely separated by heavily populated and cleared land, the panda cannot migrate.

Even if these reticent animals become desperate enough to cross the bare and inhabited areas that separate their remaining habitats, it would be difficult for them to survive the trip. Because of their inefficient digestion of bamboo, pandas cannot go much longer than five or six hours without eating.

In this series
of photographs,
Hua-Hua, a panda
that was taken into
captivity for unknown
reasons, is released
back into the wild.
Researcher
Ken Johnson joined a
team of local farmers
and members of the
Wolong Reserve staff
in an all day effort to
return the animal to
the exact spot where
he was captured.

Another danger in having the panda population and habitat so widely separated into pockets is that each species has a minimum number of animals considered to be a viable breeding population in the wild. When numbers fall below this minimum, the gene pool becomes too limited, and inbreeding produces weak animals with reduced fertility, higher mortality, and decreased resistance to disease. Such a population soon dies off. While an exact figure hasn't been set, a population of twenty or fewer pandas is considered to be in danger. For long-term survival, the minimum number is many times that—possibly one hundred.

Currently, more than half the pandas in China live in the twelve nature reserves, but only about one-fourth to one-third of the 5,922 square miles (15,338 square kilometers) these cover is suitable habitat. This means that even inside the reserves the pandas are isolated into separate groups. There are estimated to be about thirty populations within the reserves, most with fewer than fifty animals and some with as few as ten. Even in Wolong, the model reserve, there is an island population cut off from the rest of the pandas.

In places where there are enough pandas to keep the gene pool diverse, pandas do not reproduce enough to increase their population—or even, it seems, to maintain it. A 1978

Clockwise From Top Left: 1) For the first part of the journey Hua-Hua was carried up an old railroad bed in an iron cage attached to two poles. 2) The strength of several men was needed to carry the animal in short spurts up the steep slope. 3) Hua-Hua was later anesthetized and tied to a stretcher that could be carried the rest of the way on remote mountain foot trails. 4) Ear-tagged and equipped with a radio collar so researchers could track his movements, Hua-Hua was re-leased. He readapted to the wild success-fully and exhibited normal panda behavior patterns during the two and a half years of subsequent monitoring. This photograph was taken five minutes before he got up and ran off.

(Right) The hotel at the Wolong Reserve. (Far right) A patrol team dismantling a poacher's camp on a remote mountain ridge. Poachers visit these temporary camps every few weeks while they check their snare lines. They will also shoot animals when given the opportunity. Besides giant pandas, they kill musk deer and black bears, both of which contribute important ingredients to traditional Chinese medicines.

survey in Wolong determined that only eight of the twenty-one pandas observed came into heat and mated; only one cub is known to have survived. Not every panda mates, not every mating results in pregnancy, not every pregnancy results in a live cub, and not every cub survives infancy. When a cub does survive, the mother misses the next mating season because she is still caring for the baby. Odds are heavily against the female panda raising the absolute maximum of one offspring every two years.

Although predators are not a problem for healthy adults, parasites are. Roundworms are common and can clog the intestines and cause perforations in their walls. As many as 70 percent of wild pandas are thought to be affected, and although the worms are not always fatal, they retard growth and energy and inhibit reproduction. While zoos can keep pandas free of these with medication, there is no way to treat wild populations.

If the decline and fragmentation of the panda's habitat is the most significant long-term danger, then poaching is the most threatening in the short term. For no amount of reforestation will help if those new forests, like the existing ones, are full of snares. Although the panda has no place in the Chinese pharmacopoeia, it frequently is caught in snares meant for the musk deer. Until a few years ago this inadvertent snaring was the extent of panda poaching, but recently a market for panda pelts has sprung up in Japan, where the furs are highly prized. Whenever there is a market willing to pay a price high enough, someone will try to supply it.

Poaching of other animals on the reserves has been common practice for some time. The market in Che'ng-tu is full of pelts of the protected golden monkey and snow leopard, as well as the scent glands of the musk deer. The stronger the laws to protect all these animals have become, the higher the prices have become, and the more temptation there is to take the risk.

In 1988 Chinese authorities conducted a search in the villages of Szechwan's panda regions and found over 100 panda skins. Inside China, the price for one skin is equal to about eight years' wages for an urban factory worker. For a rural peasant, the value is well over ten years' wages. Skins are reportedly bringing even more exorbitant amounts in Japan. As the Japanese market increases both in price and in demand, poaching increases despite Chinese laws which now permit the death penalty. In 1987, members of a panda poaching syndicate were convicted and sentenced to life imprisonment. Two of the poachers involved in the 1988 Szechwan raid were sentenced to death.

But the reserves are so poorly patrolled that poachers are caught only after the panda is dead, if at all. The reserves are not fenced, and the terrain is so rugged that effective patrolling is very difficult. Snares, however, *are* visible in the reserves, including Wolong, where

A young panda in the Che'ng-du Zoo in China. Though the captive panda population in China is approximately 100 animals, successful births are still very rare.

there is a larger and more active field staff. George Schaller reported in *OMNI* magazine, "When I visited the Jiuzhaigou Reserve in 1983, I saw so many snares, I was surprised to see any pandas left at all."

Efforts to protect the panda have brought about another danger, one which George Schaller and others consider quite serious. Says Schaller:

> China holds too many pandas in captivity—about 100. The breeding record of these captives is dismal; two or three births a year, usually as a result of artificial insemination. Scattered in zoos and other facilities, the pandas are not part of any coordinated breeding program.

Without a self-sustaining Chinese zoo population, replacements for pandas that die in captivity are coming from the wild. The zoo animals are scattered all over China, with no program to see that they are brought together for mating. Males and females in a single facility are often incompatible, and no attempt is made to exchange them. In addition, more pandas are being captured for zoos, and many pandas "rescued" from the wild during bamboo die-backs have never been reintroduced to their old habitats.

Even the elaborate new Wolong breeding facility has had little success—only one panda has been born there since 1983. Zoo pandas and breeding programs in China are administered by a variety of government agencies with different priorities, and there is no one agency to make sure they work together for the best interests of the pandas.

Quan, one of the ten to twelve pandas living in the Wolong Reserve semi-wild breeding facility at any given time.

© World Wildlife Fund/Don Reid

Chris Elliot of the World Wide Fund for Nature also feels that China should be doing more to establish a captive breeding program instead of capturing more pandas. In *Buzzworm: The Environmental Journal* (Winter 1989), Elliot observes that China already has enough captive animals to create an effective program. "Let's make a lot of effort to get the zoos together, to do research on captive breeding methods and try to breed the animals as effectively as possible, using those animals and not taking any more from the wild."

© Sharon Cummings

"There is still a
strong faction in
the conservation
community that feels
the only way to save
the species is to pull
them out of the wild
and use technology to
preserve the gene
pool. Unless we
can serve the
entire biological
community that an
animal is part of, we
haven't truly achieved
conservation."

—Ken Johnson

# PANDAS IN COURT

In 1988, the issue of captive breeding as well as the matter of zoo demand and the pressure it places on wild populations became the catalyst for a lawsuit that tore the zoo community asunder. The World Wildlife Fund (WWF) and the American Association of Zoological Parks and Aquariums (AAZPA) brought suit jointly against the U.S. Fish and Wildlife Service (FWS) to invalidate the permit they had issued allowing the loan of a pair of pandas to the Toledo, Ohio Zoo.

The WWF cited the Convention on International Trade in Endangered Species of Wild Flora and Fauna (known as the CITES treaty), which prohibits import or export of pandas for primarily commercial purposes and further requires both the importing and exporting countries to scientifically determine that the shipment will not jeopardize the survival of the species.

"To our knowledge, such findings have not been made for most of China's exhibition loans to foreign zoos," said William K. Reilly, then president of WWF. While the federal court did not rescind the permit and stop the exhibit, which was already under way at the time of the hearing, the judge did rule that the Toledo Zoo could not

Yong-Yong, a female
on loan to the
Bronx Zoo, reportedly
came into heat with
no opportunity to
breed while in
New York.

charge extra admission to see the pandas, even though the funds were to be earmarked for conservation activities in China.

The issue was whether zoos, in their enthusiasm for panda loans, were contributing to the species' demise. The WWF, by attempting to stop the Toledo loan, was attempting to force the Fish and Wildlife Service to take a closer look at loans of all protected animals to be sure that the loan was consistent with the best long-term interests of the species.

The WWF cited a loan the previous year to the Bronx Zoo, when a female panda of breeding age came into heat during the loan period with no opportunity for either natural or artificial insemination. "What was a breeding-age female panda doing alone in New York during mating season?" concerned conservationists had asked at the time. The answer appeared to be that New York Mayor Ed Koch had put a good deal of political pressure on the Chinese to send a panda to the Bronx, and they had responded without regard to the loan animal's breeding status. The WWF asked its question again when the Chinese announced that the pair of pandas they had planned to send to Toledo were too old to travel and that they were substituting a breeding-age pair. Not only that, but the pandas had been taken from the Wolong breeding facility in violation of China's declared policy.

Officials at the Toledo Zoo felt that the WWF and AAZPA had singled out their zoo from all the other zoos with panda loan negotiations in progress and filed suit only after the zoo already had spent considerable money preparing for the exhibit. In China, diplomatic fur was rubbed the wrong way. The Chinese felt that WWF, which had been working with them to establish the breeding program, was now accusing them of profiteering and telling them how to run the breeding facility.

The Toledo Zoo had proposed a cooperative program through which Toledo would "adopt" two reserves and exchange scientific and management personnel to work on relocating people living within them. This and other educational programs in China were to be funded with the receipts from the panda exhibit. The loan was more, they insisted, than a quick rent-a-panda scheme to bring in revenue for the zoo. Moreover, by the time the Chinese decided to send breeding-

age pandas, everything was in place on both sides and the zoo didn't feel it had the right to dictate policy to the Chinese.

The Chinese Embassy in Washington defended the Chinese decision and took umbrage at the WWF's additional implication that the Chinese were not using the money they received from panda loans to further panda conservation.

"We see the pandas as ambassadors," said the embassy spokesman, Dai Xing, reminding the WWF that China had spent $25 million on panda

conservation programs. To say that the Chinese people had not used that money, as well as a lot more of their own to save the panda, was not justified, he added. China then announced that there would be no more loans of *any* pandas to the United States, thus giving up the money such loans would have generated in the future.

Clearly the Chinese were offended and unable to understand that they had become embroiled in an internal difference of opinion involving nongovernmental organizations. Westerners such as

Don Reid of the University of Calgary who have worked with the Chinese in this area are concerned that the Chinese don't understand our legal system and thought that *they* were being taken to court and tried without being given a chance to defend themselves. Many observers blame the WWF for not explaining to the Chinese what the suit was about.

There is no clearcut consensus among Western conservationists. George Schaller commented that he considered the WWF stand "excessively negative." Instead of banning loans, he suggested, the WWF should seek to limit them both in total number and to pandas not able to reproduce. Funds, he believes, should be used to provide help and knowhow to improve panda management.

The Fish and Wildlife Service, in denying a loan request that followed soon after Toledo's, cited the concern that loan revenues were not being used for habitat protection but to build more captive breeding facilities that would take even more pandas out of the wild. Of the several animals involved in loan programs both in the United States and in Europe, it noted, only two were bred in captivity. The rest had come from the wild. "We manage for wild species first," the Fish and Wildlife Service spokesman said, indicating that in the future the FWS will investigate the entire circumstances of a species in the wild before allowing permits that might encourage the

further depletion of wild animals for display in zoos.

While Toledo was understandably reluctant to tell China that they would not accept breeding-age pandas, the Calgary Zoo did exactly that with positive results. Just before the opening of the 1988 Olympic Games, Peter Karsten of the Calgary Zoo, having already committed $1.5 million to promotion of the upcoming panda loan and preparatory renovation of the zoo's facilities, was notified that China was sending a breeding-age pair. He wired China that this was unacceptable, stating further that if they did send the younger pandas, Calgary would have to keep them until breeding was complete and the offspring raised.

The Chinese, who are very nervous about foreign zoos breeding their pandas, sent a non-breeding pair, and everyone at the Calgary Zoo resumed breathing.

Short-term panda loans have become increasingly popular. They are a source of hard currency for China that can be used for conservation activities; an opportunity for huge profits for the hosting zoos, which may also contribute to conservation; and they provide public education about the animal's plight. Conservationists believe that animals potentially capable of reproducing should not be on the touring circuit.

© Sharon Cummings

© Okapia/Photo Researchers, Inc.

A giant panda in the Che'ng-du Zoo in China. "The Chinese will probably save the panda," says George Schaller, "They are determined to do it. But it has to be a long-term effort. You can never let go." "The process will not be successful without a lot of foreign assistance," adds Don Reid, "Financial assistance of course, but technical and political support as well. We must show the Chinese that giant pandas are important to people around the world."

# WHAT IS BEING DONE TO SAVE THE PANDA?

With all the conflicting opinion on how best to save the panda, it is perhaps best to focus on how effective current efforts are.

The first and most important step was the establishment of nature reserves over much of the panda's natural habitat and the development of research stations. China's own contribution to this effort has been significant—they have spent the equivalent of twenty-five million U.S. dollars—and it has been assisted by the World Wildlife Fund. Since 1980, the Fund has spent nearly four million dollars on the China Conservation Program. They have sponsored field research by George Schaller, Don Reid and Ken Johnson, and their Chinese colleagues; a captive breeding facility and research center; a panda population and habitat survey; and other management, planning, and training programs.

Meanwhile, the Chinese have worked to develop better captive breeding methods, especially by artificial insemination, as have other zoos outside of China.

Since 1949, the panda has been protected against hunting under Chinese laws. More recently, stiff penalties—including death—have been imposed on poachers and those who harm pandas, and rewards have been granted for those who help to save them. The Chinese have undertaken a massive educational campaign designed to generate public interest and help; it is already proving successful. Villagers have let stray pandas stay in village enclosures and have even set up watches to guard a sick panda against predators.

China's concern is such that the country has as many people employed in activities directly related to the preservation of pandas as there are pandas themselves. For a developing nation with other pressing demands on its resources, this is a major commitment.

In cooperation with the World Wildlife Fund, the Chinese Ministry of Forestry has developed a comprehensive management strategy to protect panda habitats. The plan calls for stricter

anti-poaching enforcement with guard posts, increased patrols, and the marking of reserve borders. In addition to the reserves, the plan establishes panda management ranges where hunting, grazing, agriculture, burning, and human settlement are forbidden. Areas which have been cleared of trees by logging operations will be reforested with bamboo. In panda habitats outside the reserves, new human settlement would be prohibited and forest cover maintained. Migration corridors are to be established and reforested to link small, isolated panda populations.

An AAZPA Panda Task Force has been established under the direction of Ed Schmidt of Chicago's Brookfield Zoo. Schmidt and Dr. Devra Kleiman of Washington, D.C.'s National Zoo went to China in October 1988 for a week-long program that Schmidt describes as an effort "to develop a dialogue with the Chinese to establish a responsible breeding program both inside and outside China." Like George Schaller, Schmidt gives high priority to this goal. "We're trying to stimulate the development of a studbook for all the captive pandas in China. Dr. Kleiman and a colleague at the London Zoo now jointly keep the studbook for pandas outside of China, but we have to establish these records where the major captive breeding population is."

## THE DILEMMA: PANDAS IN THE WILD OR PANDAS IN ZOOS?

The whole question of zoo loan programs raises an even larger one: Should creatures so rare in the wild, especially those of breeding age, be in zoos and captive programs at all? Some professionals say they should not be in zoos, citing the difficulties in captive reproduction and the already dangerously low gene pools in the wild. Others feel the only hope for survival may be in captivity and point to Père David's deer, which exist today only because the species had been preserved in European zoos.

If survival depended upon captive births since Su Lin left China, the panda would already be extinct. Captive breeding of pandas has relied upon the capture of animals from the wild, even creating a continual demand for capturing more, others argue.

The information gathered in responsible zoos forms a good deal of what we know about panda

"Animals in Chinese art are often portrayed quite apart from their natural environment," says Don Reid, "Very few Chinese can go to the mountains or experience anything wild.  So there seems to be a much stronger cultural identity with pandas as objects for display—in either paintings or in zoos. Many Chinese people sincerely believe that the animals are actually safer in zoos than in the wild. Their concept of conservation is often quite different than a Westerner's."

habits and reproduction—but at what cost? And how valid is that information for animals in the wild? If we have learned so much in zoos, why can't we breed pandas there as well as they reproduce naturally in the wild?

Nearly everyone outside China agrees that the breeding potential of the enormous number of captive pandas in China (as compared to total population) is being wasted. Since there is little or no cooperation between zoos or agencies responsible for captive animals, these institutions make no attempt to find compatible mating partners for their animals. Most captive pandas in China spend their lives in solitary confinement without the opportunity to breed. As one American zoo official put it, when a healthy panda misses a

breeding season, it's the same as losing a panda. Yet every spring, pandas all over China are without mates.

For all the differing opinions on how we can most effectively help preserve and restore the panda population, everyone agrees on certain priorities. The first of these is protection of the panda's wild habitat. Wild pandas are now living in unnatural isolation, leaving them prey to the ravages of both inbreeding and poaching. Elimination of poaching is the most immediate priority, or all the other questions will soon become academic.

Apparently, enough rugged mountain areas to support even an increased wild population still exist—if poaching and timber cutting can be con-

© Norman Myers/Bruce Coleman Inc.

trolled and lower connecting slopes can be refor-ested to encourage the mixing of populations. In such a situation, the periodic bamboo die-backs could actually benefit the panda (as perhaps they did historically) by forcing the animals to move about and mix with other populations, keeping the gene pool viable. But, as the recent manage-ment plan outlines, the reserves need to be patrolled, and new varieties of bamboo with stag-gered flowering cycles should be introduced.

In some areas, corridors of bamboo and forest cover could be planted to connect isolated high-land populations. The question no one is pre-pared to answer about these corridors is how to get the conservative, homebody pandas, who are not concerned with matters such as gene pools, to use them.

More research needs to be conducted on the genetic status of wild pandas. Such a study was initiated in 1986 by the Chinese and the WWF to evaluate genetic diversity. The study's goal is to collect blood samples and compare genetic vari-ants, thus determining the degree to which vari-ous wild populations and the population as a

(Top) Another panda pair enjoying a meal at the Canton Zoo. (Bottom) A panda in the Wolong breeding center. "Captive breeding should be only one part of an integrated approach to saving pandas. Sufficient numbers of pandas exist in captivity to establish a cooperative captive breeding program without the need to remove additional pandas from the wild."

—Ken Johnson

© World Wildlife Fund/Don Reid

© Sharon Cummings

whole have become inbred. Based on these findings, reserve managers may need to use aggressive outbreeding techniques, such as relocation, to keep the gene pool viable.

What to do with captive populations is an area that produces less agreement. Some experts would release all the pandas rescued during the bamboo die-backs, mixing them into new populations if possible. Certainly the drain on wild populations in support of zoo exhibits must end. New captures should be limited to pandas that are legitimately rescued such as orphaned cubs.

Loans to zoos should be limited entirely to captive-bred pandas known to be past breeding age, except for loans made to establish breeding programs at zoos. "To disrupt the routine of ani-

mals by shifting them repeatedly to different facilities with different foods and climates causes stress to the pandas and can disrupt future reproductive activity of both subadults and adults," says George Schaller. If there is any chance of breeding an animal, it should be given every opportunity.

Schaller also feels that breeding efforts should concentrate on getting animals into the wild, where they can and will breed more easily. He points to the "dismal" record of Chinese zoos and the absence of any coordinated breeding program. China should spend less money on elaborate breeding facilities and instead move animals back into the wild, at least until the willingness to cooperate among zoos is in place.

Some others feel that, at least until wild habi-

tats can be secured and connected, more emphasis should be placed on captive breeding in China. The technology for artificial insemination, fetal transplants, and frozen storage of sperm and ova exists. Dr. Betsy Dresser, Cincinnati Zoo's reproductive physiologist for endangered species states, "If we don't do something *now* with all these reproductive technologies, or just with captive natural breeding, we're not going to know enough when the real crisis hits." In this fast-paced field, every day brings new advances, and many reproductive scientists agree with Dresser. As long as the genetic material exists, they feel, there is always hope.

But almost everyone outside China agrees that such artificial means are at best a fallback position. Most successful breeding is natural, but Dr. Terry Maple, Director of Zoo Atlanta points out the problems of trying to tell the Chinese how to run their program. "From their point of view," he remarks in *Buzzworm*, "the U.S.A. is hapless with its poor results in Washington, and it is a great source of pride to them that the Chinese can produce baby pandas." What they don't seem to see, he goes on to note, is that the United States has had only two pandas to work with, while China has dozens.

Everyone outside of China, and even some scientists inside, agree that China's efforts are poorly coordinated and riddled with bureaucratic attitudes. Tang Xiyang, in his *Living Treasures: An Odyssey through China's Extraordinary Nature Preserves*, points out that "the many agencies now employed in the conservation, study, breeding and exhibition of the giant panda [in China] are not sufficiently integrated. Even in a single department, communication is sometimes minimal; much work is wastefully duplicated because colleagues do not exchange ideas or share experiences." He quotes a colleague as saying that the only hope of saving the giant panda is in the modernizing of China. But can the panda wait?

All of these differences of opinion bring us to a basic problem of wildlife conservation: Whose

"With collective wisdom and dedication we must assure the panda a future. We can only hope that the choices made today are the correct ones, that the research and conservation efforts will forever preserve the animal in its mist-shrouded mountain home."

—*The Giant Pandas of Wolong* by George Schaller, Hu Jinchu, Pan Wenshi, and Zhu Jing.

GIANT PANDAS ⌇ SAN DIEGO ZOO ⌇ 1987–1988

animals are they? Do pandas—or any other endangered species—belong to the country they live in, or to future generations of the world as a whole? Are they China's to save, sell, loan, propagate, or allow to die? If they are not, how do we tell China that, especially in the face of their own substantial efforts on the panda's behalf? And, as a practical matter, what are we going to do if the Chinese tell us to mind our own business.

Conversely, what would we say to another nation that made a similar claim upon our diminishing mineral resources or upon our natural supply of Alaskan oil? Natural resources, no matter how rare or threatened or symbolic, have always belonged to whoever occupied the land they were on.

Pandas involve a lot of politics, especially since China sees them as the symbol of their friendship with other countries and the World Wildlife Fund sees them as its logo. Each would be seriously embarrassed by a failure to save the panda. But beyond the symbolic, diplomatic, and even conservation considerations, who does have the final word on the panda's fate?

If efforts in China are to succeed and international wildlife groups are to continue their support in a constructive way, each side needs to get its house in order. China needs to get the various responsible ministries working together, and Western groups need to settle their disagreements among themselves and use their energy and funds in the most constructive way possible.

The groundwork for such a plan was laid in the summer of 1987 when China hosted an International Conference on Wildlife Conservation, cochaired by the respective presidents of the National Wildlife Federation and the World Wildlife Fund. The conference included hundreds of Chinese wildlife experts and more than fifty others from eighteen countries. With a basis for discussion established, and with the WWF's research and financial commitment, an atmosphere of international collaboration toward a common goal is in place.

Another international concern is that of cooperation between zoos outside of China over

© Sharon Cummings

breeding programs. Until recently, such coopera-tion has always been on a one-to-one basis, as between London and Moscow or London and Madrid.

But when Mexico City's male panda died, Lon-don Zoo Director David Jones offered Chia-Chia for a breeding loan. For London to give up its star attraction for so long was a farsighted gesture typ-ical of London's concern for the greater problem of creating a viable breeding program outside of China. Unfortunately, Mexico City's panda facility was straining at the seams, and without funds to expand it, the director there had to turn down the London offer.

At this point, the Cincinnati Zoo stepped in and suggested that Chia-Chia stop over there. All the fees generated by his exhibition would go to Mex-ico City for the new facility and for its breeding programs.

This solution neatly addressed the belief of many conservationists that there ought to be a major breeding facility outside China. By concen-trating all breeding programs—both wild and captive—in China, they worry, the entire future of the species is subject to potential hazards. A disaster, political, environmental, or in the form of disease, could wipe out the Chinese panda population.

Some conservationists even advocate exploring the possibility of a large, secure panda reserve outside of China in a fenced and patrolled high-land environment as much like the original habi-tat as possible (such wild areas exist in South and Central America). Pandas could be rotated for optimum breeding, genetic diversity, and avail-ability of compatible mates. This strategy has been called, variously, a silly idea and a unique, creative concept.

"The future of humankind is threatened less by pollution, food shortages, and depletion of oil and minerals...than by the exponential destruction of the earth's natural environments, by the extermination of species. Each death of an animal or plant represents another broken link in the chain of life, a glorious and irreplaceable past not only slipping away and depriving generations to come of their heritage but also creating a downward spiral in the diversity of life that may ultimately have disastrous consequences."

—*The Giant Pandas of Wolong*

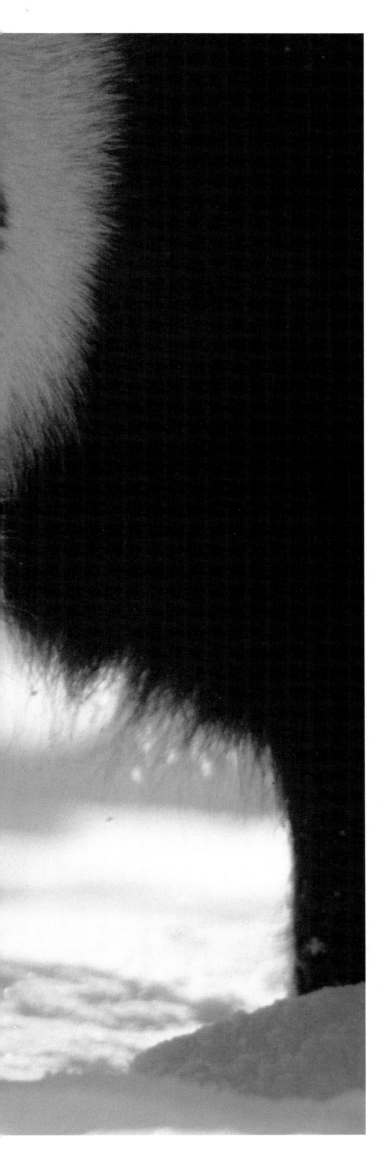

# A SYMBOL FOR THE WORLD

The specter of a panda population so diminished that it spends its final days on earth munching bamboo (or barbecued chicken) in captivity haunts everyone who works with pandas. George Schaller calls it his nightmare. Captivity, artificial breeding techniques, and other programs that take animals from the wild or support them outside their native habitats are last-ditch stands at best. Or they are stopgap measures to solve short-term problems, such as bamboo die-backs, or to keep open long-range options, as in the case of sperm banks.

Preserving the panda in any long-term sense means preserving its habitat. Without the habitat there will be no panda population. As England's Prince Philip, president of the World Wide Fund for Nature wrote in the book *Down to Earth*:

> It may seem that all is not lost while it is possible to breed pandas in captivity. All may not be lost, but is there really much point in maintaining a captive population if there is no prospect whatever of reintroducing them to their natural habitat because in the meanwhile it has simply disappeared?

The problem of the panda, while largely in China's hands, is not China's alone; everyone who cares about the loss of a species is involved. Although it will take commitment in China and diplomacy internationally, the panda will be saved only by everyone working together.

As Prince Philip goes on to say in *Down to Earth*, "The situation of the giant panda in western China illustrates virtually all the problems confronting the world of living nature."

The panda is not only a symbol but an indicator of the present degree of cooperation possible among countries: If the various governments and conservation groups involved can work together to solve the problem of the panda and its habitat, then there is hope that these same governments and organizations can muster the same cooperation to save other habitats and focus on worldwide environmental threats.

"When we talk about giant pandas as a resource, we reduce wildlife conservation around the world to a black and white issue. Sure we need to work toward their preservation in terms of economic betterment, but really, at the end of the day, they mean much more than dollars and cents. They touch our spirit in a much more fundamental way— hence their ability to evoke such wonder and awe."

—Don Reid

# INDEX

*Names of individual pandas are given in italics. Italicized page numbers refer to captions and pictures.*